MW00568441

Cats

This is a Parragon Book
First published in 2002

Parragon
Queen Street House
4 Queen Street
Bath BA1 1HE, UK

Copyright © Parragon 2002

ISBN: 0-75258-255-0

The right of Paddy Cutts to be identified as the author of this work has been
asserted in accordance with Section 77 of the Copyright, Designs and Patents Act
of 1988.

Editorial, design and layout by Essential Books,
 7 Stuceley Place, London NW1 8NS

Photographs © Animals Unlimited/Paddy Cutts

Printed and bound in China

Cats

Paddy Cutts

Contents

Introduction

Available in many different shapes, colours and fur lengths, cats are today in the same league as dogs when it comes to popularity as domestic pets.

This, sadly, was not always the case; the feline has in fact had a rather chequered career. In early civilizations dogs were useful for herding and guarding but the humble cat was not generally regarded as a creature of value until the Ancient Egyptians recognized its worth. For the Egyptians grain was a most valuable commodity, as it provided nutrition when made into flour and bread. Rats were always a problem in granaries, and so the cat's usefulness as a ratter was soon appreciated – cats were the answer to the simple problem of no grain = no food. From then on the cat became a prized possession and its status improved considerably, so much so that cats came to be regarded as gods; the punishment for killing a cat was the death sentence. When a cat died it was afforded a full burial ceremony, just like the pharaohs, and today the British Museum in London houses literally thousands of mummified cats retrieved from these early Egyptian tombs.

The Exotic Shorthair has the body of a Persian without the long fur – this is a Blue Cream Colourpointed Exotic

Other civilizations held the cat in equally high esteem: in the Far East they were regarded as sacred, often to be found guarding Buddhist temples; in Japan the Mi-Ke was thought to be a symbol of good luck; and in Norse legends Freya was another much-worshipped cat.

In the Middle Ages, however, the popularity of cats took a serious dive. Black cats were considered to be witches' close friends or 'familiars' and, along with the witch, were burned alive at the stake. It was not until Victorian times that the cat really regained popularity, and it was during this period that the Cat Fancy formally came into being.

With the advent of the Industrial Revolution, foreign travel became a more feasible proposition for many people. The British became a nation of great seafarers, and travelled the world. Cats were an important part of life at sea, as they were needed to keep the rat population down on board ship.

It soon became evident that cats in far-flung parts of the world were quite different to the tabbies, torties and blacks seen in Britain; in warm locations, such as Southeast Asia, cats tended to have short, sleek, pale-

Originating in Canada, the Sphynx is at the other end of the scale, since it has only a limited amount of fur

coloured coats with darker points, while in the colder Arctic regions they had thick, double coats. These two climates gave rise to the breeds we now recognize respectively as the Siamese and Russian Blue.

It was also noted that deformed tails were very common in the Far East, particularly in Japan, and this gave rise to the Japanese Bobtail and, probably, the Manx – the latter most likely having been a stowaway that 'jumped ship'. The Irish Sea can be exceedingly stormy and ships often used to stop off on the Isle of Man, awaiting calmer seas, before docking in Liverpool.

From the cold, upland area of Anatolia in Turkey came a semi-longhaired cat with a thick undercoat, white body and auburn markings, which is now known as the Turkish Van. And from Persia (now Iran) came the luxuriantly coated longhaired variety. This glamorous creature – the Persian – was popular then and still is today.

Although cats are known to have been exhibited at country fairs from the 1500s, the first 'official' cat show is generally regarded to be the one that took place at the Crystal Palace, south London, on 13 July 1871. The show had an amazing entry of 170 cats, classified as either

Introduction

Longhair or Shorthair, and with Tabbies, Persians and the 'Royal Cat of Siam' (Siamese) having the most entries.

Shortly after, the National Cat Club was formed to establish a record of parentage. This august institution still exists today, but only as a club that holds an annual show in London in December. Other clubs were formed and, in the 1920s, a central registrating body was set up to keep all records of pedigrees. This was the Governing Council of the Cat Fancy (GCCF).

How things have changed from these humble beginnings. Today the Cat Fancy is active worldwide; in the UK there are now seven different show/registrating sections: Longhair (Persian), Semi-Longhair, British Shorthair, Foreign Shorthair, Oriental, Burmese and Siamese. Some of the breeds, such as the Siamese, Burmese, Russian Blue and Norwegian Forest Cat, are original, emanating from the countries that are reflected in their names. Others, such as the Bengal and Snowshoe, have been 'genetically manufactured' by breeders who wished to create a new variety.

Some cats have been created by accident. The Burmilla, which gave rise to the whole spectrum of Asian cats, and the Ocicat, which resulted when an American breeder attempted to produce an Abyssinian-pointed Siamese, are two prime examples. Even as this book is being written, new breeds are being accepted; the Cat Fancy is always changing and it's almost impossible for any new breed book to be completely up to date.

All of these groups are quite distinct. The Persian type is often described as 'cobby', which means a solid, stout cat with a compact overall look. British Shorthairs are usually described in the same way, as the body size and shape is quite similar to that of the Persian. Both of these groups are short faced and, when very snub nosed, often referred to as being of 'extreme' type. The Semi-Longhairs, Foreign Shorthairs and Burmese are 'middle-of-the-range' sorts of cats, as they display no extreme features. Siamese and Orientals are at the other end of the scale from the Persians; these are lean, lithe and angular cats, with long snouts and large ears. Therefore, the short-faced Persian and the long-nosed Siamese represent the most 'extreme' of types possible within the accepted cat breeds.

The Cat Fancy originated in the UK, and the original Standard of Points was drawn up from this. However, there are subtle variations in both breed names and classification between the UK and US. For the purposes of this book, therefore, the British standards as recognized by the GCCF are referred to, and where US terminology is different this is pointed out in the main text (in brackets over main breed heading).

As with any specialist subject, cat terminology can be quite specific, so where necessary reference should be made to the Glossary at the back of this book.

The Tortie-Tabby Pointed Colourpoint is an example of how clever breeders can design a new colour and pattern

Why cats make good pets

What are you looking for when choosing a pet? A subservient, fawning creature that will obey your every command? If so, go for a dog. Cats are quite different, and will only accept you on *their* terms. If this idea sounds appealing, then read on. There are so many different sorts of cat available – all with quite different characters – that there is bound to be one that will fit your lifestyle and settle happily into your household.

So why do they make such good pets?

- Compared to some pets, such as dogs, cats are relatively small and do not require a tremendous amount of space within the home. They will adapt equally as well to living in a flat or apartment as they will to being in a house with a garden, especially if introduced to their new home as a kitten.

- Cats are generally undemanding as their attitude to life is that they are 'their own cat'. Having said that, some breeds, in particular the longer-haired varieties, do need their owners to devote a certain amount of time to grooming.

Introduction

- The foreign and Oriental breeds love to play and interact within a family situation and this is why so many cat owners find these breeds so enchanting.

- Some breeds, especially Siamese and Burmese, love to chat, and enjoy conversations with their owners.

- Cats are generally clean creatures and do not need to be house-trained. Given a litter tray they are unlikely to defecate elsewhere, and mothers instinctively teach small kittens to use their trays.

- Cats do not need to be taken for walks twice a day – they just exercise themselves (sometimes to the detriment of the household furnishings).

- It has been scientifically proven that cats lower your blood pressure – stroking a cat on your lap causes the cat to purr, and this purr reverberates through your body, giving a soothing effect. Indeed, more and more hospitals are welcoming a visit from a sick patient's cat, as it seems to both aid and speed recovery.

- Cats may seem aloof and distant, but once they have accepted you – on their own terms – you will have a pet that trusts you and will be loyal and loving. This is a uniquely feline trait that any owner will find rewarding.

Persian kittens, like this little Pewter, are cute – but remember when they grow up their thick coats will need time for grooming

- Elderly and/or disabled people benefit greatly from cat ownership. Cats particularly suit people who may not be able to walk for any great distance, and so cannot easily own a dog.
- A cat will ensure that its owner gets up in the morning, as it will demand to be fed. If the owner is asleep, the cat will ensure a fast awakening by way of early morning licking, pummelling (pudding making) and purring – enough to get anyone up and about.

Introduction

Cats are thespians – sensitive creatures that have much in common with actors, artists and musicians. These are innovative animals that are able to improvise and busk their way through life – they are survivors!

There is a lovely quotation that summarizes the cat: 'The difference between cats and dogs is that dogs come when called and cats take a message and get back to you.'

The number of breeds available is always increasing, and the Snowshoe is one of the newer varieties

How to choose a cat

Choosing a cat usually means weighing up a number of options. Take time to think about the questions below and you'll be well placed to find the sort of cat that will fit in with your home and lifestyle.

Remember that a cat can live for a serious length of time, so you should really think about owning one of these delightful creatures in a way not dissimilar to how you would think about starting a human family. A cat, barring accident or illness, may well live to eighteen years of age or more – the same length of time the average child would remain in his or her parents' home. Yes, owning a cat is a lifelong commitment, but an incredibly rewarding one if you make sure you select the right cat for you in the first place.

Do you want a cat or a kitten?

- Would you prefer a pedigree cat, i.e. one of well-recorded parentage which is registered with a recognized governing body, or would you be happy with a moggie, where you may well know little or nothing about its family history?

Introduction

- Would you accept a 'rescue' cat that has been abandoned or maltreated and, a bit like a second-hand car, can be either amazingly reliable or really let you down?
- Would you accept an older cat? Senior-citizen felines can make the most delightful pets, and will not be as boisterous or demanding as kittens.

A kitten is almost always the first choice for families with young children but do remember that kittens grow up very quickly. Although kittens are officially recognized as adult cats when they reach the age of nine months, some breeds are rather precocious and will want to mate much earlier. Siamese and Burmese are well known for this and it is not uncommon for siblings of these breeds to mate together at an early age. Therefore, it is most important to get them neutered.

Pedigree kittens can be quite expensive – be prepared to pay £250 and upwards, depending on the breed in question. If you have approached a well-known breeder, or indeed had one recommended to you via a breed club, the sum you part with should provide you with a kitten that is representative of its breed not only physically but also in terms of temperament. For this price, you can expect your kitten to be registered with the appropriate governing body (for which a certificate should be provided by the breeder), be fully inoculated, and preferably insured.

If you want an adult pedigree cat, rather than a kitten, look to the local breed group (any of the registrating bodies have contact information on their websites – see

Smoke Persians display the maximum of colour graduating to only a slight amount of pale undercoat

page 190). This way you may well acquire a pedigree cat for a fraction of the cost of a kitten, or even for free. You may be asked to make a contribution towards the cost of neutering/spaying and inoculations.

Non-pedigree cats are always available in sanctuaries and animal shelters. These can become the most rewarding of pets. Often they will have been pretty badly treated and will take time to settle in to a normal domestic environment. But the rewards – a hissy, spitty creature that turns into an adoring lap cat – cannot be overestimated. When they eventually trust their new owner, their love says it all.

As you read though this book you will realize that there is a huge selection of pedigree breeds available – some demanding of your time with their grooming requirements and others simply demanding of your presence. Read on, the decision is yours.

Grooming

Cats have varying lengths of fur, and therefore quite different grooming requirements. In the main text stars (* to *****) denote the level of grooming needed.

Starting at the top of the scale (*****) are the heavily coated Persians (or Longhairs), the fur of which needs regular attention. It would be unwise to take a cat of this variety on board if you were not prepared to devote *at least* ten to fifteen minutes to grooming every day. Think of it as a regular regime, something you can do while watching your favourite television programme, for example. A Persian that is left ungroomed is not a thing of beauty; its coat will start to mat and this will cause it great discomfort. In fact, your cat may even end up at the vet's surgery undergoing a general anaesthetic – unpleasant for the cat and expensive for the owner. If you think of matted fur in a similar way to an old rusty car you will begin to understand – once rust sets in it just spreads. It is easy to keep a longhaired cat in good condition if a simple course of action is followed. Most pedigree Persians will have been used to this procedure from early kittenhood and will enjoy daily grooming.

Introduction

- Brush and comb the coat, ensuring that any tangles are removed and paying special attention to the hind-quarters, tummy and under the chin, as these are the areas that are most likely to get knotted and matted.
- If you notice any knotted parts, remove them with the aid of blunt-tipped scissors, cutting gently towards the matted part without cutting the skin.
- Use talcum powder to bulk up the fur and act as a 'dry shampoo' to remove any dirt and grease from the coat.

The Semi-Longhairs (* * * *) do not usually need this level of attention, but will still benefit from regular grooming. British Shorthairs (* * * *), particularly the Manx, have dense coats and should also be frequently groomed.

Foreign Shorthairs, Burmese, Siamese and Orientals (* to * * *) are the least demanding in terms of grooming but a weekly brush and comb should keep their coats in good condition.

Cats are generally thought of as creatures that hate water, but there are occasions when they need to be bathed. This is usually for show purposes, particularly to keep a white- or pale-coloured cat looking perfect.

The Birman is a popular variety of Semi-Longhair, and the Cream Point is one of the newer colour additions

However, any cat may require washing at some point. Accidents can happen. Cats are fond of getting under cars and sump oil is not healthy for them. Always make sure, therefore, that you wash your cat if it has come into contact with oil or any other potentially harmful substance. Follow these steps:

- Run luke-warm water into a washbasin or a baby bath in the bath (anything that is suitably cat sized and will make them feel secure).

Introduction

- Use a special cat shampoo, or one that is designated as safe for babies.
- Lather well, and rinse off.
- With longhaired varieties, apply hair conditioner. This will help release any knotted fur.
- Give a final rinse.
- Wrap the cat in a towel and dry the damp fur. If your cat lets you, use a hairdryer.

Shorthaired cats can benefit from a bran bath, which is a much more simple procedure:

- Take a couple of handfuls of bran and warm them in the oven.
- Spread the bran liberally over the cat's coat and rub in well.
- Brush out and your cat will have a lovely, clean coat free of dirt and grease.

Essential equipment

Before you introduce your new cat or kitten into your home, there are a few essential items you will need to buy:

Cat carrier

In order to bring your cat home, you will need a sturdy carrying box. Unless you are considering showing your cat, this will not usually be your most frequently used piece of equipment – it is usually brought out only for the annual trip to the vet for booster inoculations, and to and from the boarding cattery when you go on holiday. Cat carriers come in all shapes and sizes, and with different price tags to match (see Travelling and boarding, page 33), so shop around for one that best suits your needs.

Litter tray

These come in many forms, from the simple, shallow pan to 'high-tech' covered trays. Some even have deodorizing filters and use 'washable' litter that can be re-used. If your cat mostly uses the garden for its toilet, then a simple tray could be offered for night-time use. Choose one with high sides so that the cat does not shower the litter everywhere. If the cat is confined to the home, or several cats are to share the same tray, it is worth investing in something more durable – a large tray with a covered lid would be best. Again, have a look around the local pet store and see what's available.

Litter and scoop

Although sand, wood shavings and even garden soil were long used as litter, these days many varieties of special cat litter may be found on the market. These are generally either 'clumping', or 'non-clumping'. With the former the litter will clump around the waste matter, which means it can then easily be removed with a scoop. The clean litter remains, which is then topped up. With the latter the whole tray must be changed after use. Fuller's Earth-based litter is probably the most commonly used litter, but it is heavy to carry and tends to 'powder', resulting in a lot of dust and particles. Mineral-formulated litter is lighter, does not powder and usually contains a de-odorizer. This is the most popular type with owners whose cats are confined to indoors.

Food and water bowls

Cats will eat off anything (some showing a distinct preference for fine bone china) but it is more hygienic to have separate utensils for cats and humans. Cat bowls are plastic (cheap, unbreakable, but chewable and not long-lasting), earthenware (solid, non-tippable, but breakable) or metal (the most expensive, but virtually indestructible and able to be sterilized in boiling water). Double bowls are available, so water and food can be in one convenient place, and there are even time-controlled bowls, the lids of which will open at a pre-set time. The latter are useful in hot countries, where flies will attack food if it is left out, or for cats with certain medical conditions, such as diabetes, where food has to be offered at regular intervals.

Beds and bedding

Given the opportunity, most cats will opt for their owners' bed as the most suitable sleeping accommodation. But not everyone wants a furry, purring hot-water bottle as a bed companion. Choose a cat bed with high sides, to keep out draughts, and provide ample blankets for the cat to snuggle under. For complete luxury, heated beds can be bought (useful for elderly or sick cats that need to be kept constantly warm) and there are even 'Radiator' beds – a recent innovation that offers a cosy, fur-fabric nest with clips that hang over the top of the radiator!

Toys and scratching post

Cats love to play, and a good selection of toys should be provided. A visit to the pet store will reveal a huge range. However, the good old catnip mouse is still the favourite with most cats. Why not try making cat toys at home? Cats love rattling sounds, and a 35mm film canister filled with rice can provide hours of entertainment. Cats naturally scratch their claws to keep them sharp so invest in a cat scratching post to protect your furniture and carpets from damage.

Collars and tags

If your cat is to be allowed access to the world outside your garden, it is important that it should be identifiable if it gets lost. Although modern microchip technology can provide an electronic tag implanted under the skin – or a registration number tattooed in the ears – a collar with a tag inscribed with *your* (not the cat's) name, address and telephone number is an obvious and perfectly adequate form of identification. Tags sometimes fall off, so make sure that you print your postcode in indelible ink on the inside of the collar too.

Cat runs and chalets

If you wish your cat to have access, together with a certain amount of freedom within the garden, then a cat chalet incorporating a run could be the answer. There are several specialist companies that provide these, most of which advertise in the various cat journals (see page 191). If your garden is relatively small you might also consider 'cat proofing' the whole area. This involves using chicken wire or a similar wire. Attach the wire to batons fixed to the existing fences or walls and extend it upwards to make a total height of at least six and a half feet. The wire should then be *loosely* rolled inwards towards the garden, and stiffened with a support. This way, if the cat tries to jump up onto the wire, the wire will bend in a downward direction, and the cat won't be able to get over to the other side of the fence.

Feeding and nutrition

At the turn of the century cats were usually fed on table scraps, which supplemented the prey they naturally caught and ate. Today things are somewhat different and feline nutrition is big business, with many manufacturers vying for a share of this vast market. The range of foods available means that every type of feline palate is catered for, as well as age group, size and medical needs. Generally, cat food is available in two forms:

The outgoing and intelligent Abyssinian is a cat often referred to as ancient, as it closely resembles the mummified cats found in Egyptian tombs

Wet/semi-moist foods

These are sold in tins, punnets and pouches. To both human and feline, they look and smell appealing, and come in a wide array of flavours. On the downside, their high moisture content means they can quickly become contaminated in hot climates unless consumed quickly. Some breeds, especially the Persian Longhairs, tend to be intolerant of this type of food and it gives them tummy upsets and diarrhoea.

Dried-/hydrolyzed-protein diets

Convenient to serve and longer-lasting, these are a complete food sold in a bag or carton. They may look rather boring to you but your cat will find them tasty and they provide all the essential ingredients it needs for a healthy, balanced diet.

Unlike dogs, for which an even larger variety of pre-prepared food is marketed, cats do not vary greatly in size. On the supermarket shelf there are usually three types of cat food to be found:

Kitten food

A high-protein diet that ensures a kitten gets plenty of the nourishment that a growing animal needs.

Adult maintenance

The basic diet that will keep any cat active and healthy.

Less active/older cat

These foods are formulated for cats that are not as active as they were in their prime, and are aimed at providing maximum nutrients without causing an unhealthy increase in weight.

All tastes are catered for, even vegetarian and organic, although these tend to be only available from specialist stores. Lastly, and crucially, there are foods designed for a variety of 'special diets'. These are usually available only from veterinary practices after a clinical diagnosis has been made. Cats are prone to kidney problems in older age and these 'science' diets can help an elderly cat remain healthy and happy for a few more years.

*The Russian Blue is an old-established and indigenous breed
originating from the port of Arkangel'sk*

Many owners find that a balance of both wet and dry
foods works well. Try out a few options and see what
seems best for your cat. But you may as well resign
yourself to the fact that your cat will always think the best
meal is what *you* have on your plate!

Introduction

Travelling and boarding

These are really two quite distinct factors regarding sensible and responsible cat ownership, but that have one thing in common – a cat carrier.

Travelling with a cat

It is not sensible to travel with a cat loose in a car, so the obvious solution is to contain the feline in a carrying box. For most short journeys a simple and cheap container, such as a wicker or wire-mesh basket, or a polypropylene carrier, will suffice. These are not tremendously durable, but should work well if not overly used. If you show your cat, a much sturdier carrier will be needed (the vetting procedure in queues can last quite a time, and in winter the cat will become chilled if it is not in a well-insulated carrier). There are cat carriers that will convert into a bed, which are handy if you frequently move your cat, and sturdy carriers that fold conveniently flat for storage.

If you're taking your cat on board a plane you'll find that most airlines will insist on certain requirements in terms of carrying. Some air companies will even provide the necessary container, albeit at extra cost.

Boarding

When you go on holiday your cat will often be forced into having a holiday as well (unless you are lucky enough to have a neighbour who is happy to feed and attend to your cat's needs). Boarding catteries will usually only accept cats that are neutered and that have their booster inoculations up-to-date. This is sensible – would you wish to expose your precious cat to other cats that might carry a virus?

Always view the cattery first in order to be quite sure that you are happy for your cat to stay there. Don't be afraid to ask questions: Do the owners live on the premises? Is there a vet in regular attendance? And always seek references – well-respected catteries will be delighted to provide these.

When booking your cattery, think of it in the same terms as you would your own holiday – leave it too late and there won't be any accommodation left. Some well-regarded catteries can be booked up as much as a year in advance so always think ahead, particularly if you are going away during the really busy seasons, such as Christmas, Easter and the school holidays.

About this book

There is a vast number of different types of cat. Due to their almost infinite variety, their classification is quite a complex business. Many types of cat differ from others within their specific group only in terms of colouring and/or pattern.

Of the seven groups featured here, by necessity five contain a Variations section. These are the Persians, the British Shorthairs, the Oriental Shorthairs, the Burmese and the Siamese. The Origins, Appearance, Temperament and Suitability as a Pet sections are applicable to all of the cats within each of these groups, but their colouring or patternation varies as described.

Cat breeds are grouped together according to the lines set out by the GCCF, except where it was felt to be more logical to group them by coat length.

Persian group (Longhairs)

With their long, luxuriant coats, large, expressive eyes and sweet natures, Persians are instantly recognizable and it's not surprising that this breed is the most popular pedigree breed in the world today. Stars of stage and screen, these glamorous cats just ooze class!

The Persian was by no means the first longhaired breed to be brought into the UK. This accolade goes to the Angora, a breed that was first seen in the city of Ankara, Turkey, from whence it gained its name. In Victorian times, when foreign travel became more common, a much more heavily coated cat was discovered

With their huge, expressive eyes, it is hardly surprising that the Persian is such a popular variety. This Golden Persian sums it all up!

in distant Persia (now Iran) and this usurped the popularity of the Angora, which faded into oblivion until it was 're-created' in the 1960s.

In general, most modern-day Persians conform to a similar Standard of Points, with a few slight differences. Structured breeding programmes have resulted in a quite mind-boggling number of colours and patterns within this general group, including Colourpoints (a Persian with a Siamese-patterned coat) and what must seem an anomaly, the Exotic Shorthair, a new variety that has all the type and form of the Persian, but with a shorthaired coat!

The most important factor to consider when contemplating owning a Persian is how much time you have available. These sweet-natured cats are undemanding of your personal attention, being quite happy to laze about for most of the day. However, they do need serious attention paid to their long coats and will require grooming for at least ten minutes a day to ensure that they stay in pristine condition. A Persian with a matted coat is a sad sight indeed – uncomfortable for the cat and expensive for the owner when neglect means a trip to the local grooming parlour.

Origins Although it is thought that longhaired cats were brought to Europe as early as the seventeenth century, it was not until the late 1800s that any form of Standard of Points was drawn up or, indeed, details of parentage recorded. Early Persians included the patterned tabbies, as well as the self-coloured Blue – reputedly a favourite of Queen Victoria. Other, short-haired, breeds were seen at the early cat shows of this era, but none commanded as much attention and popularity as the Persian – a status that it retains today.

Appearance Over the years, the appearance of the Persian has changed quite radically. The cats seen in Victorian times had quite elongated faces and, although the coats were long, the fur was neither as thick or luxuriant as it is today. Current standards call for a well-muscled, medium-sized, elegant, cobby cat. The short face with full, round cheeks and large, lustrous eyes (most typically of deep copper, though some variations require other hues) give the Persian its appealing expression. The legs are short and stocky and the tail short and bushy. The most distinctive feature of the Persian is the coat, which should be long, thick but fine

Colourpoint (Himalayan) Persians are 'designer' cats with the Persian's long coat and Siamese's restricted pattern

in texture with a fullness around the chest and neck. A huge range of colours and patterns is available. In general, the varieties can be summed up as self (or solid), non-self (patterned, colourpoint and shaded) and – the odd-one-out – shorthaired, also known as the Exotic.

Temperament Sweet natured, gentle and quiet-voiced, the Persian in general is not a particularly athletic breed or one that will demand your constant attention. These cats are natural 'lounge lizards'. Posing is second nature to them.

Suitability as a pet With their somewhat laid-back attitude to life, the Persian should suit most households. There is very little by way of aggression in their personality and they love an easy life. While they will enjoy playful games, they will not *demand* them in the same way that a Foreign Shorthair or an Oriental would (see pages 104 and 138), and, within reason, do not mind being left when the owner is at work – they will probably just sleep. With their easy-going nature, they usually fit in well with dogs and other pets. They are only 'high-maintenance' in terms of their grooming. If you cannot afford to put the time aside for a daily regime but still like the look of the Persian, you might be happier with the shorthaired version, the Exotic (see page 61).

Grooming: * * * * *
Origin: Persia (Iran)
Activity: *
GCCF Group: Longhair (Persian)

Variations

Black

A dense black, solid to the roots, with no sign of 'rustiness', although it is acceptable for kittens to show faint 'ghost' tabby markings until about six months old.

Left This Black Persian kitten shows all the signs of success on the show bench – indeed, she went on to become a champion

Right Deep copper eyes set off against deep, black fur ensure that the Black Persian is always high in the popularity stakes

Blue

A delicate, even, pale grey that should not show any obvious shadings or markings.

Left It is not unusual for Persian kittens to go through a woolly 'ugly duckling' stage when they are younger

Above But in maturity, with a full coat, they soon turn into beautiful swans!

Cream

In the 1900s, these were often thought of as poorly coloured Reds, but the current Cream, with its pale-to-medium coat, is one of the most popular varieties today.

Left The delicate pale cream colour, offset against the complementary deep copper eyes, makes this a most attractive variety

Below The cream colour should be sound throughout the coat, without any sign of a white undercoat. This one fits the standards perfectly

Red

One of the earlier-known colours, the Red is hard to breed without some slight 'ghosting'. For this reason, although the deep, rich-red colour should be as sound as possible without tabby markings, some slight shading is acceptable on the forehead and legs.

Left With the red variety some slight, deeper shading of colour is sometimes seen on the forehead, but this is quite permissible

Right With their thick coats, it is quite natural for Persians to moult in the warmer months; despite the lack of 'ruff' this cat still shows good type

Chocolate

A newer variety that has arrived by the breeding programme devised to produce the Colourpoint (see page 55), the Chocolate has a warm, medium-to-dark-chocolate coat, which should be free of shadings or markings.

Left Although a more recent colour variation, the Chocolate is rapidly gaining popularity

Right Highly 'colour co-ordinated', Chocolate Persians even have chocolate nose leather and paw pads to match their coat

Lilac

Another by-product of the Colourpoint breeding programme (see page 55), the Lilac is an attractive shade of pinkish, dove grey.

Left The delicate colouring of the Lilac Persian makes this a most attractive addition to this group of cats

Right For perfection the coat should be of a sound and even colour, as this cat well displays

White

This colour requires a pure white coat with no shading or marks. The eyes, unlike those of most Persians, may be blue, orange or odd (one blue and one orange eye).

Left It is often said that blue-eyed white cats are deaf, but this is not true of the pedigree varieties

Left White Persians can have three different types of eye colour, and this odd-eyed white has one blue- and one copper-coloured eye

Bi-colour

A mixture of any of the accepted solid colours and white, both of which should be clearly defined. In some cat fancies it is preferred to have an inverted 'V' of white extending from between the ears to the top of the nose.

Left This Blue Bi-colour shows the perfect facial marking of the classic inverted white V

Below A popular colour variation, the Cream and White Bi-colour Persian should have the typically luxuriant coat

Blue Cream

Although a tortie-patterned breed, the Blue Cream is sometimes classified separately. The standards vary between the UK and the US. In the former the coat colours should be well intermingled, while in the latter obvious patching of colour is preferred.

Different Torties display very different patterns as these two Blue Creams show

Tabby

Available in a multitude of colours, the tabby has darker markings overlying a paler coat. Typically, these should show an 'M' marking on the forehead, 'oysters' on the flanks and a 'butterfly' over the shoulders. Often the expert eye of a judge is needed to see these subtle patterns, given the length of the coat.

Left Brown Tabby Persians have been known for years, but Silver Tabbies now have a larger following

Below The Silver Tabby is one of the most glamorous of the tabby colours and is popular worldwide

Tabby and White

A mixture of tabby with white. The tabby pattern should be more evident than the white, and the white is usually restricted to the face, underbelly and feet.

Left Tabby, intermingled with tortie colours, gives rise to the tortie-tabby and white – a multicoloured cat

Right This blue-tabby and white displays the correct standard of points, with the tabby pattern being more obvious than the white areas

Tortie Tabby

A mixture of both tortoiseshell and tabby colours and patterns – this is probably one of the most colourful breeds available!

Tortoiseshell

The 'Tortie' is usually a female-only variety – the occasional male born with this pattern is invariably sterile. Torties have a mixture of colours in their coat, based on either red or cream with overlying tones of any of the accepted self colours.

Left It is desirable, in the black tortie, for well-broken patches of red to be seen in the black coat, as this example shows well

Right No two torties ever display the same pattern, but this one conforms to the standards just as well

Tortie and White (US: Calico)

Originally called the Chintz cat in the UK, this breed is also known as the Calico in the US. The Tortie and White is a mixture of any of the recognized tortie colours overlaid on white. The ratio of pattern to white varies within the fancies from a nearly white cat with some colour to the exact opposite.

Left The white areas should be quite clearly defined from the tortie pattern, and this kitten shows super markings

Right The Black and White Tortie is often regarded as the 'classic' Calico, with its mixture of black, red and white in its coat

Colourpoint (US: Himalayan)

Essentially, these are cats of Persian type, but with a pale body colour and the restricted darker points of the Siamese, which is often referred to as the 'himalayan' pattern. Originating from breeding plans set up in the US and Sweden, the self- and tortie-pointed colours became established. Later, a breeder in the UK, Monika Forster, devised a programme to produce the tabby points. Unlike most Persians, these cats have blue eyes that recall their Siamese parentage. They tend to have a more outgoing temperament than the average Persian but are neither as lively or noisy as the Siamese.

The Colourpoint Persian, unlike most others within this group, has blue eyes like its Siamese ancestors

Self Points (US: solid)

The darker points should be evenly matched in tone to the paler body colour; available colours include all those seen for the Siamese (see page 170).

The subtle cream colour of the Cream Point is the palest of all Colourpoints and this is the UK Supreme Grand Champion

Tortie points

A mixture of any of the accepted solid colours, intermingled with red or cream.

Tabby Points (US: Lynx)

As with tabby point Siamese, the preferred pattern should display clear tabby points, with a distinct 'M' marking on the forehead. Tabby points are recognized in all the accepted colours.

Tortie Tabby Points (US: Torbie/Torby)

This variation shows the normal tabby pattern, overlaid with the richer tortie colours, including red and cream.

This young Blue Tortie Tabby Point shows great promise – beautiful markings and a super coat

Shaded

This variety incorporates those Persians that have coats of graduated shading, starting from the lightly tipped silver coat of the Chinchilla to the barely perceptible shaded undercoat of the Smoke – plus all the subtle tones that can be found in between.

Chinchilla

The most lightly shaded of all, the Chinchilla at first glance appears to be a white cat. Look again and you'll see that it has a delicate black tip to each shaft of hair, giving a shimmering, sparkling-silver effect. The distinctive large, round eyes are emerald green and 'mascara-ed' (outlined in black). The pink nose is also outlined in black. The Chinchilla is the superstar of the Persian world and is universally famous as the star of the James Bond films *You Only Live Twice*, *Diamonds Are Forever* and *On Her Majesty's Secret Service*; in the UK, the Chinchilla also found fame advertising a brand of carpet and is still often referred to as the 'Kosset Carpet Cat'!

The luxuriantly coated Chinchilla is one of the most popular varieties in the Persian group

Shaded

Slightly more heavily tipped than the Chinchilla, the Shaded was often thought of as an overly dark-shaded Chinchilla. Now available in differing colours, the original Shaded was the silver.

The Shaded Silver has been usurped in popularity by the glamorous Chinchilla

Cameo

This is a gently shaded breed that has a pale, almost white, undercoat overlaid with tips of red, cream or tortoiseshell. The overlying colour should be most obvious on the face, spine and tail.

***Right** This Cream Shaded Cameo displays all the delicate shading required of this breed*

Pewter

As its name suggests, this variety should be the colour of pewter. The coat has a pale, almost white base, but is heavily shaded with darker overtones.

More densely coated than the Chinchilla, the Pewter variety is gaining popularity all the time

Smoke

The most densely shaded of all, the Smoke only reveals its pale undercoat when it moves! Often mistaken for a solid colour, this is the subtlest of shaded colours.

Exotic shorthair

The Exotic is the stranger to this group – a shorthaired Persian! Yet the Exotic is a true Persian in type, but with a short, thick and plushy coat. Available in all the same colours and patterns as the longhaired Persian, this is a perfect breed for anyone who appreciates the appearance of a Persian but hasn't the time for the laborious grooming associated with this group.

*Available in all Persian colours and patterns, the Colourpoint (**above left**) and the Bi-colour (**above right**) are popular varieties*

Semi-Longhair group

In the early days all cats with long coats were classified as Persians. As more breeds became available, it became evident that those originating from Persia were of a quite different type from those coming from other regions; not only did the Persians have longer and thicker coats, their whole body and facial structure was different too.

As it was considered unfair to judge the lesser-coated, and often more elegant and lightly boned breeds against the solidly built Persian, a new group was introduced to encompass all longhaired cats of non-Persian type – the 'Semi-Longhairs'.

Originally, this was a small group including established breeds from far-flung corners of the world, such as the Birman from Burma and the Turkish Van from Turkey. Today it incorporates many other varieties. Some, such as the Maine Coon and Norwegian Forest Cat, are indigenous to their native countries. Others are the longhaired 'cousins' of existing shorthaired breeds, such as the Balinese (Siamese) and Somali (Abyssinian). More recently, breeds that have been 'designed' have come into this Semi-Longhairs category, the Ragdoll and the Tiffanie being good examples.

This group encompasses a vast range of cats. They differ not only in type and pattern, but in temperament. Generally, Semi-Longhairs are more active and outgoing than true Persians, but are neither as boisterous or noisy as their, often related, foreign counterparts. This is a group that enjoys attention and companionship, and appreciates both families and other pets.

Semi-Longhairs do not need as much grooming as Persians. However, they are more high maintenance in this respect than the foreign varieties.

With their distinctive white paws and sweet expressions, the Birmans are tremendously popular

Angora (US: Oriental Longhair, Javanese)

Although a rare breed, the Angora is fast growing in popularity. Available in many colours and patterns, it combines all the grace of the shorthaired Oriental breeds with a longish, silky coat and distinctive plumed tail.

Origins The Angora was originally a longhaired cat from Ankara in Turkey. Its popularity dwindled in Victorian times when Persians were imported from Iran. It was not until the 1960s that UK breeders began to 're-create' the Angora. Essentially, the breed we see today is a semi-longhaired version of the Oriental Shorthair (see page 138). In the US, some Angoras originate from true Angoras rediscovered in Ankara Zoo in 1962. These are called Turkish Angoras, to distinguish them from the re-created UK lines.

Appearance A lithe, lean, and elegant breed with long, slim legs. The eyes are almond-shaped, and should be green in all coat colours except white, where they may be blue or odd-eyed. Accepted coat colours include black, blue, chocolate, lilac, red, cream, cinnamon, caramel, fawn, shaded, smoke, tortie, tabby, silver or white.

Temperament Intelligent and companionable, the Angora loves attention. It is loud and talkative so usually gets it!

Suitability as a pet An active breed ideal for a similar household, it fits in well with children and other pets. Having a longish coat, it needs regular grooming.

*This Semi-Longhair equivalent of the Oriental Shorthair, the Angora has a silky coat well seen in the Lilac (**left**) and Silver Tabby (**right**)*

Grooming: * * * *
Origin: UK
Activity: * * * * *
GCCF group: Oriental Shorthair

Balinese (US: some colour forms called Javanese)

Basically, the Balinese is a Siamese with a semi-longhaired coat. Its grace and elegance, combined with its liveliness and intelligence, makes this an increasingly popular breed.

Origins First seen in California in the late 1940s, the Balinese was the result of a natural mutation in a litter born from two shorthaired Siamese cats. When two of these 'fluffy' Siamese were mated together they proved to breed true; all had the distinctive himalayan coat restriction so typical of Siamese, but with the added attraction of a long, silky coat. The Balinese was officially recognized in the US in 1963 but not in the UK until the 1980s.

Appearance An elegant, supple and graceful cat with long, slender legs, plumed tail and the typical Siamese wedge-shaped head with wide-set ears. The body is a pale colour, with the darker points restricted to the face, ears, paws and tail. It is seen in all colours accepted for Siamese – seal, blue, chocolate, lilac, red, cream, tortie, tabby and torbie point (the latter five colours being classified as Javanese in the US).

Semi-Longhair group

Temperament Less boisterous and vociferous than their shorthaired relative the Siamese, Balinese cats are active, intelligent and sociable.

Suitability as a pet Gregarious by nature, the Balinese enjoys the company of other pets and children. The long, silky coat requires regular grooming.

*The Balinese is considered part of the Siamese group in the UK and seen in the same range of colours including seal (**above**) and lilac (**left**)*

Grooming: * * * *
Origin: US
Activity: * * * * *
GCCF Group: Siamese

Birman

Often described as the 'sacred cat of Burma', the Birman is a unique breed with an interesting, albeit perhaps fabled, history. The whole look of this breed, with its deep blue eyes and distinctive white paws, is enchanting.

Origins Originating from Burma, this is said to have been the cat sacred to the Buddhist temples there. (The Burmese breed also lays claim to this!) The legend surrounding this ancient breed tells of a priest who lay dying in his temple. The priest's faithful cat came and rested his paws on his master's chest to offer companionship in his last moments and, when the priest died, the cat's paws turned the purest white and her eyes turned to deep, brilliant blue. The Birman was first imported into France in 1919. It increased in popularity and was eventually recognized in the UK in the 1960s.

Appearance Elegant, with a long, solidly built body, rounded head and full cheeks, its coat is its most distinctive feature. Of medium length, with a 'ruff' around the neck, it is pale, with darker himalayan points on the face, ears, tail and legs, but with white paws and beautiful blue eyes.

Temperament Sweet natured, relatively quiet-voiced and not over-demanding, the Birman is a friendly and affectionate companion.

Suitability as a pet This breed suits any family and relates well to other pets, but does not like being left on its own if the family is out for most of the day. Also, regular grooming is needed.

*The Tortie (**above**) is a recent additions to the Birman breed while the original Seal (**left**) retains its appeal*

Grooming: * * * *
Origin: Burma
Activity: * * * *
GCCF Group: Semi-Longhairs

Maine Coon

Often considered the original 'all-American breed', but with a possible French connection, the Maine Coon is generally regarded as the largest breed of cat. A big, friendly purring machine, it makes a super pet.

Origins The generally accepted story is that the original Maine Coons were seen in the State of Maine in the US, hence the first part of their name. These cats had broadly striped tails reminiscent of the tail of the raccoon, which gave rise to the other part of their name. Some people believe another story: that Maine Coons originated in France and came to America with Marie-Antoinette during the French Revolution.

Appearance A sturdily built, muscular cat with a medium-length head and large, wide-set ears. The coat is heavy, thick, dense and waterproof, with a ruff around the neck. Their ears and paws have distinctive 'tufting'. Available in all colours except himalayan, agouti, chocolate and lilac.

Temperament An undemanding breed that is both friendly and intelligent, though also independent. Its size belies its nature – this is the gentle giant of the cat world.

Suitability as a pet With its friendly and playful nature, the Maine Coon makes an ideal pet for any family, as long as time is spared to groom the coat. Ideally, the Maine Coon loves the outdoors and so is best suited to a home with a garden, but is equally happy with apartment life, provided the owners are not away for long periods of time.

Below Early
Maine Coons
were most often
Tabby and
White

Above Almost any colour is now
acceptable for the breed, including
this Red Silver and White

Grooming: * * * *
Origin: US
Activity: * * *
GCCF Group: Semi-Longhairs

Norwegian Forest Cat

A relative newcomer to the Cat Fancy, the Norwegian Forest Cat was first imported into the UK in the late 1980s, but it now has a firm following in both the rest of Europe and the US. A strong, solidly boned cat, this is an active breed renowned for its climbing abilities.

Origins Norse legends refer to a mountain-dwelling fairy cat called 'Skogatt' that could climb mountain faces unreachable by other cats. Mention is also made of beautiful, large, longhaired cats that served the goddess of love and beauty, Freya. Certainly, the Norwegian we see on the show bench today is an athletic breed with a certain ethereal quality, which suggests there may be an element of truth in these legends.

Appearance Large and well muscled, with long legs, a long, sturdy body and a triangular-shaped head with high-set, tufted ears. The coat is thick, long, glossy and waterproof and is most luxuriant around the neck and chest, the ruff, and the plumed tail. The cat may be of any colour or pattern except chocolate, lilac and himalayan pattern. The large eyes may be of any colour.

Temperament A friendly and outgoing cat, albeit quite independent. Not an overly demanding breed.

Suitability as a pet A good family pet that prefers access to a garden and trees. If it is kept indoors it needs climbing frames to keep it amused. As with any longish-haired cat, the coat will need regular grooming.

Right Norwegian Forest Cats are gaining a following in the UK. This one was a show winner

Left This Norwegian Forest Cat was one of the first imported into the UK

Grooming: * * * *
Origin: Norway
Activity: * * * *
GCCF Group: Semi-Longhairs

Ragdoll

Gentle, loving and affectionate, the Ragdoll has, undeservedly, been made fun of in the media. Breeder Anne Baker claims the breed developed when her pregnant cat suffered a fractured pelvis in a car accident. All the resulting kittens and their later progeny, she claimed, 'flopped' when handled, just like a ragdoll. This is hard to substantiate since it is unheard of for an animal's genetic make-up to be affected by a traumatic experience.

Origins The Ragdoll is thought to have arisen from mixed ancestry involving Birman, Siamese and Persian cats. They were first seen in California in the 1960s but were not imported into the UK until 1981.

Appearance Muscular, broad chested and with sturdy legs, it has a broad head with wide cheeks. The coat is dense and silky and is available in three colour patterns – Colourpointed, Mitted and Bi-colour. Each pattern may be seal, blue, chocolate or lilac.

Temperament Ragdolls are sweet and undemanding, but their name should not be taken as an invitation to throw them across the room; these cats flop on their own terms once they have confidence in their owner.

Suitability as a pet An easy-going breed that will fit well into most family situations and is happy with children and other family pets. The coat will require regular grooming. The Ragdoll's trusting, laid-back nature means it should be confined to the home or a 'cat-proofed' garden (see Cat runs and chalets, page 28).

*The Ragdoll is available in three patterns. Of those, one is the Mitted (**above**) and another the Colourpointed (**left**)*

Grooming: * * * *
Origin: US
Activity: * *
GCCF Group: Semi-Longhairs

Somali

An elegant, sweet-natured and affectionate breed. Basically, it is the semi-longhaired equivalent of the Abyssinian (see page 106). It is the occasional 'fluffy' kitten that appeared in early litters and was dismissed as a poor example of the Abyssinian breed.

Origins Although a natural mutation of the Abyssinian, these longer-coated kittens were initially ignored in the UK. This was not the case in the US. In the 1960s a far-sighted American breeder decided to breed them in their own right. Their popularity soon grew. By the late 1970s they were imported to the European mainland and, finally, to the UK in 1981. Today the Somali is an internationally popular breed.

Appearance A breed of foreign type with a firm, well-muscled body and long legs. The head has a moderate wedge, with large, wide-set and tufted ears. The coat is soft, fine and dense, and should display triple-banded ticking. The fur is more profuse around the ruff and tail, giving this breed its typical fox-like appearance. Colours include sorrel, chocolate, blue, lilac, fawn, cream, tortie – and the silver variations of all the above.

Temperament Outgoing and intelligent, Somalis love company and do not like being left on their own. That said, they do not always enjoy a crowded feline household as they appreciate plenty of one-to-one attention from their owner.

Suitability as a pet A quiet-voiced but active breed that will suit most family circumstances, especially given the opportunity to roam outdoors. The Somali is a real huntin', shootin' and fishin' cat and will often bring back little presents! Time must be spent on grooming.

*Somali cats are available in a wide range of colours – Chocolate (**left**) and Lilac (**right**) are some of the newer variations*

Grooming: * * * *
Origin: US
Activity: * * * * *
GCCF Group: Semi-Longhairs

Tiffanie (US: Tiffany)

A semi-longhaired cat of Burmese shape, the Tiffanie is an increasingly popular breed that combines the intelligent, outgoing personality of the Burmese with the more refined character of the Longhairs. There is a lack of consistency between UK and US terminology; in the former the Tiffanie is part of the Asian (Burmilla) group (see page 114) while in the latter it is thought of as a semi-longhaired Burmese.

Origins In the UK the Tiffanie is the result of a mating between a Burmese and a Chinchilla Longhair in the 1980s. A structured breeding programme was created by the original Burmilla breeder, Baroness von Kirchberg. In the US, the Tiffany does not have a well-documented ancestry, hence the slight difference in spelling, to avoid any confusion.

Appearance The Tiffanie is elegant and muscular with the balanced proportions of the Burmese. The coat is long, fine and silky. This should be most noticeable around the neck and tail. It is available in a dazzling array of colours and patterns: black, blue, chocolate, lilac, red, cream, caramel, apricot and the associated torties and tabbies. These can also be shaded, smoke, silver, and with either full or Burmese expression.

Semi-Longhair group

Temperament Intelligent, friendly, affectionate and outgoing, the Tiffanie (as with all cats of the Asian/Burmilla breed) is unusual in that 'temperament' is written into its Standard of Points. This cat was not just bred for beauty but for its gentle and loving nature too.

Suitability as a pet Loving and loyal, this quiet-voiced cat makes an ideal family pet. Regular grooming is necessary. If this is a problem, look to acquiring a Burmilla or Asian.

Tiffanies are Semi-Longhairs from the Asian/Burmilla group. The above are both brown, but left is the paler variety and right is the Smoke

Grooming: ****
Origin: UK
Activity: ****
GCCF Group: Foreign Shorthairs

Turkish Van

Betraying an unusual trait for felines, this breed loves water and is often referred to as the 'swimming cat'. It is an ancient breed that has more or less escaped human intervention and is the result of generations of natural, local matings – plus a helping hand from Ankara Zoo.

Origins This is a truly Turkish cat that comes from the eastern, upland area of Anatolia around Lake Van. These origins gave the breed its fondness for water. It likes to swim. To save it from extinction Ankara Zoo set up a breeding programme to protect the gene lines, some of which have been imported back into the UK.

Appearance A sturdy, long-bodied and muscular breed, with strong legs and neat, tufted paws. The head is wedge-shaped with high-set, well-feathered ears. The coat is long, silky, soft and chalk-white, apart from the distinctive Van pattern on the head, which should incorporate a white blaze, ears and tail. Classically, the Turkish Van is a white cat with auburn points and amber eyes; today they are seen with amber, blue or odd eyes and coat colours can include cream, black, blue, tortie, tabby and pure white.

Semi-Longhair group

Temperament Sweet natured, friendly and intelligent, this is a sociable cat with a quiet voice.

Suitability as a pet This breed will enjoy living with a family, especially one that has a pond or a swimming pool. Otherwise, a regular dip in the bath might suffice for these water addicts. Regular grooming is essential, particularly in the winter when the coat is denser.

Right The classic Turkish Van is usually regarded as auburn. This cat has won supreme best in show at both the National and Supreme cat shows in the UK

Left Newer colour variations include the Black Turkish Van

Grooming: * * * *
Origin: Turkey
Activity: * * *
GCCF Group: Semi-Longhairs

British Shorthair group (including US and European)

It is difficult to say precisely when 'domestic' cats first arrived in Britain. One school of thought suggests that the breed we now call the British Shorthair arrived in this country with the invading Roman troops, somewhere between the first and fourth century AD. Another suggestion is that they are simply a domesticated variety of the indigenous wild cat, which still exists today but is rarely seen outside of the Scottish highlands. Even there, the numbers are rapidly diminishing.

When cat shows first became popular the most commonly coloured shorthairs were white, black, black and white and tabby. Frances Simpson wrote of these cats in her 1911 book *Cats for Pleasure and Profit* that, 'It seems almost a pity to so far encourage these cats as to give classes for them at our Shows (*sic*).' Little did she realize how popular this variety would become. What she dismissed as a humble, 'common' cat today ranks second only to the Persian in registration figures and is available in a multitude of different colours and patterns. It is undoubtedly a well-respected and acknowledged breed worldwide. The only variety in this group that impressed Frances Simpson in any way was the Manx – currently the least numerous of any of the recognized breeds. How times have changed!

The British Shorthair has seen many changes since these early days and today appears to bear little resemblance to the native moggie. Over the years breeders have sought to improve type, and this has given a compact, chunky and cobby cat that is also the breed most often chosen to advertise cat food.

The Red Spotted Tabby has a coat with distinctive red spots overlaid on a paler base colour

Sweet natured and affectionate, British Shorthairs have been eloquently described by one breeder of these cats as 'the next best thing to a fireside moggie'! With their thick, plush coats and rounded shape they are the real teddy bears of the cat world.

Origins The gene for short hair dominates over that for long hair – most 'mongrel' cats have short fur – and this helps explain the origins of the modern pedigree British Shorthair. Similarly short-coated cats are found throughout the rest of Europe and in the US, and have

The British Colourpointed arrived by way of a cross between British Shorthairs and Persians. The woolly coat of its ancestors is still in evidence in this first-generation example

British Shorthair group

The male British tend to have obvious jowls, as this Blue Bi-colour stud cat displays

given rise to the European and American Shorthairs. Along with the imported Persian and Siamese breeds, these indigenous shorthairs were first seen at the early cat shows that took place at the turn of the nineteenth century and they provided the basic gene pool for the breed that is now recognized as the British Shorthair.

Appearance This is a chunky, sturdy and muscular breed, the males being noticeably larger than the females. The British has a broad chest, with short, stocky legs and a short, round-tipped tail. The head is broad and well rounded, with small, neat, wide-set ears.

Male British should also show distinct 'jowls' around the cheeks. The eyes are large and lustrous, usually a deep orange or copper colour, reflecting the coat colour (though there are some exceptions). The coat is short, crisp, dense and plush (except in the case of the Manx – see page 102). The overall look of the British should be of a cobby cat, but without the extreme facial conformation of the Persian or Exotic.

Differing from the general standards for most British cats, the Manx is unique in that show specimens do not have a tail

British Shorthair group

Temperament 'Laid-back' pretty much sums up this breed, though there are some exceptions, such as the Silver Tabbies and Colourpointed varieties. The British is not one of the most active of pedigree breeds. Some might even call it lazy. In general, these are big, friendly, purring machines that will like nothing better than to doze on a comfy lap.

Suitability as a pet British make an ideal pet for any household as nothing seems to faze them. They are equally at home with a single person as with a household full of other pets and children. They are low maintenance, as they don't demand constant attention and entertainment. However, their dense coats shed quite heavily, especially in the warmer months, so they do require regular grooming. This is especially so in the case of the Manx, which has an unusual double coat.

Grooming: * * * *
Origin: UK (US)
Activity: * *
GCCF Group: British Shorthairs

Variations

Black

A glossy, deep jet black that is solid to the roots and with no trace of rustiness, shading or white hairs.

Left A true Self variety, the British Black kitten has the same dense black coat as the adult

Below The black coat and amber eyes of this variation make for a striking combination

Blue

A medium-to-light blue, without any trace of silvering or shading.

Left The British Blue is the best known colour variation in this group

Below Although cute and cuddly as kittens, the British tend to become very large in adulthood

Cream

This is one of the more difficult coat colours to breed and retain a clear coat, as most will display some amount of tabby ghosting; an even, pale-toned cream is the required colour, with as few markings as possible.

Left This Cream displays the 'cobby' shape desired of the breed

Below It is not easy to breed a clear-coated Cream, but this is close to the mark

Chocolate

A more recent development, this colour originated as a by-product of the Colourpointed breeding programme (see page 55), and still often carries the restricted Himalayan gene for this pattern. Recognized in its own right, this variety has an attractive, warm, rich and even chocolate-coloured coat.

Left One of the rarer colours, the Chocolate is gradually establishing a following

Below The coat should be of even colour as is the one seen here

Lilac

As with the Chocolate, this is another variety originating from the Colourpointed programme. The coat is an even, pinky-tinged, frosty grey.

Left Although Lilac is one of the newest variations, this male show the correct headshape for a British

Right The female British is smaller and less muscular than the male

White

This variety should have a coat that is pure, brilliant white, with no sign of yellowing or any other markings (although slight head shading is acceptable in kittens). The White is recognized in three distinct eye colours – blue, orange or odd-eyed (one blue and one orange eye).

*British Whites have three acceptable eye colours, two of which are (**left**) odd-eyed and (**below**) orange eyed*

Bi-colour

A two-tone cat that is a well-defined mixture of white and any of the recognized self colours.

Left The Cream Bi-colour is a most popular variety and is not always easy to breed without some markings

Above *The striking contrast between blue and white makes the British Blue Bi-colour a very stylish cat indeed*

Tabby

Tabbies are one of the oldest-known varieties of cat, originally seen as either brown or red. Today these colours are rarely seen, as the more glamorous silvers have become more sought-after and thus more popular. The latter are usually more elegant and less heavily boned than the original colours.

Left The classic Silver Tabby should have well-defined markings, including 'oyster' markings on the flanks

Right The Silver Spotted Tabby is one of the most glamorous cats in this group

Tortie

The most popular of this variety is probably the Blue-Cream, a delicate and well-mingled mixture of these two colours. Torties are now recognized in any of the accepted self colours, mixed with red and cream.

Right The Tortie was first seen as a mixture of black and both rich and pale red. This example shows a well-balanced pattern of colour

Left The body should display well-intermingled colours

Tortie and White (US: Calico)

This variety was produced by mating a Tortie with a Bi-colour. As with the Torties, their colour variations are recognized in all the accepted self colours.

Left The Blue Cream and White is an attractive mixture of blue and cream, with white patches

Right The Black Tortie and White has a coat of both rich and pale red, and black interspersed with clearly defined patches of white

Smoke

Sister to the very lightly shaded British Tipped (opposite), the Smoke has a darker coat shading down to a pale under-mantle, which is only revealed when the coat is stroked. Best-known in the black variety, the Smoke may be of any of the main self colours accepted for this breed.

Left With a well-mingled coat, the smoke shading is more difficult to see in the Torties

Below The silver undercoat of the Black Smoke subtly distinguishes it from the Self Black

Tipped

This is basically the British Shorthair equivalent to the well-known Chinchilla Longhair. The undercoat is pure white, classically overlaid with black tips, which gives this breed its sparkling appearance. Other, less dramatic, colours are now acceptable. The green eyes have a 'mascara-ed' effect and the lids are outlined in black. This is echoed on the nose, which is pink in colour but with a distinctive black edging.

Left Just like the Chinchilla, the British Tipped should have eyes well defined with a black 'mascara' effect and a brick red nose, also outlined in black

Right The Black Tipped British has a white under coat with just the tips of the fur coloured in black, giving a sparkling effect

Colourpointed

As distinct from the Colourpoint Persians, in this group the term Colourpointed is used to describe British Shorthairs that display a coat with the restricted himalayan coat pattern. The British Colourpointed is the result of mating British Shorthairs with Persian Colourpoints, as the latter were more true to the type required. This resulted in some of the early British

These Blue Tortie (left) and Blue (right) Colourpointed kittens show a little of the 'fluffiness' of their Persian relations

Today, the Colourpoints have exactly the same type as the other British cats, as the Chocolate Pointed clearly shows

Colourpointed having somewhat fluffy coats, but this trait has been eradicated through selective breeding programmes. As with any cat with this restricted coat pattern, the British Colourpointed has blue eyes and may display any of the colours and patterns accepted for the Siamese.

Manx

Although this is classed as a British Shorthair, the Manx is quite unique, having a type, character and temperament distinct to other breeds within this group. To most this is the 'tailess' cat. In the most correct form for judging purposes this is quite true, but they also come in other forms, some with tails more apparent than others.

Regarded as the traditional cat of the Isle of Man, an island situated in the Irish Sea off the west coast of England, the Manx is thought to have arrived in the UK with sailors returning from the Far East. Cats with deformed tails are well recorded in the Orient, particularly the Japanese Bobtail, so it would not be surprising if the Manx did originate from these lands.

For show perfection the Manx should not show any vestige of a tail

Tailed Manx also exist, and are useful in perpetuating a strong and healthy breed

Today the Manx has three tail lengths: Rumpy, the generally accepted variety, with a non-perceptible tail and a dip at the spine's base; Stumpy (or Rumpy Riser), with a small, vestigial, amount of tail; and the tailed variety, with a full tail. Only the Rumpy is accepted as a show specimen, although the other types are accepted for breeding.

What all three types display is the typical Manx body conformation of the rear legs being longer than the front ones, which gives rise to the typical rabbit-like gait.

This breed is accepted in all colours and patterns except himalayan.

Grooming is essential for this breed, as they have a double waterproof coat; unless regularly groomed, the Manx will 'mat' more than any other shorthaired variety.

Foreign Shorthair group

This group has the largest range of different breeds. If an active, intelligent and unusual shorthaired cat appeals to you, this is the section you should concentrate on. Originally, the Foreign Shorthair section of the Cat Fancy included all cats of 'foreign' shape, including the Siamese and Burmese, but these, along with the more recently developed Orientals, now have their own separate classes in shows.

What is so interesting about the Foreigns is that they all have a quite different attitude to life and some are far more outgoing than others. The artificially, and accidentally, created Burmilla (and the associated Asian cats) even have 'temperament' included in their Standard of Points. The Bengals were specially bred to mimic the coat of the wild Asian Leopard Cat, but with the gentle nature of the domestic cat. The Rex varieties, Devon and Cornish in particular, are the result of natural mutations first seen in these counties of the UK, and their impish personality ensures they stay high in popularity.

New varieties are constantly being created, mainly in

Foreign Shorthair group

Ocicats are available in a variety of colours, including tawny, chocolate and black silver

the US, though these are not usually accepted in other countries. Often breeds designed by breeders in order to make a quick profit, these are usually cats of extreme and undesirable type. The best publicized is the highly controversial Munchkin (a cat of dachshund-like proportions with very short legs).

Abyssinian

One of the earlier-known shorthaired breeds, the Abyssinian has changed little over the years, except that it is now available in a range of colours. The agouti coat, typically with at least four bands of colour, makes this an attractive breed, and one that is recognized worldwide.

Origins Thought to have been brought to the UK from Ethiopia by British soldiers returning from the Anglo-Abyssinian war of the 1800s, the Abyssinian was nicknamed the 'bunny cat', the colouring of its coat being similar to that of a wild rabbit. African origin is also suggested by the vast collection of mummified cats from Egyptian tombs that bear a striking resemblance to the breed. By the late 1880s they were recognized in the UK but were not imported into the US until 1907.

Appearance An elegant breed with long, slender legs and a tapering tail. The head is wedge-shaped with large, tufted ears and large, almond-shaped, wide-set eyes. The dense, short, close-lying coat is finely textured and firm. The original agouti ticking pattern is now seen in sorrel, blue, chocolate, lilac, fawn, red and cream, as well as the torties and silvers of these base colours.

Foreign Shorthair group

Temperament Friendly and intelligent, these cats enjoy both feline and human company and do not like being left on their own for any great length of time.

Suitability as a pet Generally, the loyal and loving Abyssinian fits in with most domestic situations. However, they do not like being overcrowded with other cats and do not always accept other breeds readily. Their short coats require little by way of grooming.

*The original colour of Abyssinian was the Usual (**right**), but today it comes in many colours, including Fawn (**left**)*

Grooming: **
Origin: Ethiopia (Abyssinia)
Activity: ****
GCCF Group: Foreign Shorthairs

Asian

The term Asian, as distinct from the Burmilla, Tiffanie and Bombay, covers all those other colours and patterns arising from the original Burmilla breeding programme (see page 114). Sweet natured and graceful, they are a popular addition to the Cat Fancy.

Origins The Asians are another by-product of the original mating between a self-coated Burmese and a tipped Chinchilla. It was always understood that a multitude of colours and patterns would eventually result, but this did not happen for several generations of breeding. As these new cats were of foreign (i.e. Burmese) type, it was decided that a suitably oriental name should be found to encompass the whole group.

Appearance All Asians are essentially cats of Burmese type, but with different coat patterns and colours. They are medium-sized and well-muscled, with wedge-shaped heads and medium-sized, wide-set ears. Colours include black, blue, chocolate, lilac, caramel, red, cream, apricot, and the associated tortie and tabby patterns, and smoke; these are also accepted in silver and standard versions in both Burmese and full expression.

Foreign Shorthair group

Temperament Intelligent, friendly, playful and athletic, the Asian is a breed that will suit most domestic environments.

Suitability as a pet Active and talkative, Asians relate well to a family situation and enjoy the company of cats and other animals. Their short coats require little grooming but their lively, playful nature means they need regular company at home.

This Apricot Ticked Tabby Asian shows all the elegance that is required of this breed

Grooming: * *
Origin: UK
Activity: * * * *
GCCF Group: Foreign Shorthairs

Bengal

A newer breed, at the time of writing this is the sixth-rated breed on the UK registration list, and is recognized worldwide. It has been bred to combine the appearance of a wild cat with the sweet nature of the domestic feline.

Origins In the US in the 1960s a domestic short-hair female cat and a male Asian Leopard Cat, a small wild cat, were mated. The Bengal was difficult to establish, as males from the first generation were infertile. By the 1980s early problems had been overcome by outcrossing to other breeds of similar body shape and size, and a careful breeding programme ensured that the 'wild cat' coat pattern and texture was retained.

Appearance This is a large, muscular breed, with the hindquarters slightly higher than the shoulders. The rounded head has prominent whisker pads and small, wide-set ears, rounded to the tips. Unique to this breed are its unusually soft coat texture and its patterns, which may be spotted or marbled. The original varieties were Brown Bengal, with a mixture of black markings and shades of brown that almost glitter, and the paler, dilute Snow Bengal, with the same patterns but in grey.

Foreign Shorthair group

Temperament Friendly, intelligent and companionable, its nature is similar to that of the Burmese, though the Bengal's voice is quieter, with a very distinctive 'chirrup'.

Suitability as a pet Generally, this active breed will enjoy the stimulus of a busy household and will get on well with other pets and children. One quirk in their character – they love water and like to have a dripping tap left on for them to enjoy!

Right The Bengal is seen in two patterns, the Spotted, which shows clearly defined spots . . .

Left . . . and the Marble, which has swirls of pattern

Grooming: * * *
Origin: US
Activity: * * * *
GCCF Group: Foreign Shorthairs

Bombay

With their sleek, black coats, and brilliant golden-yellow eyes, it is not surprising that the Bombays were nicknamed 'the patent leather kids with the copper penny eyes'. There are differences between the UK and US versions.

Origins There are two distinct origins of this breed, developed on opposing sides of the Atlantic. In the US the Bombay was the result of a planned mating in the late 1950s between a sable (UK: brown) Burmese and a black American shorthair. The objective was to create a domestic cat that resembled a black, mini-sized panther. Bombays have been recognized in the US with full status since 1976. In the UK, the Bombay is a more recent breed. It is related to the Asian group of cats.

Appearance Essentially, this is a self-black Burmese with the same type and body conformation as the Burmese (see page 154). The coat is short and close-lying but, unlike that of the Burmese, is of a solid jet black with a distinctive sheen.

Temperament Athletic, outgoing and intelligent, the Bombay is a sociable animal with an equable temperament.

Suitability as a pet Like all cats within this group, the Bombay enjoys – and demands – attention. It will thrive in an active household and does not like being left on its own without the companionship of another pet.

Right The sleek, shiny Bombay differs in origin between the US and UK

Above With a jet black coat, reminiscent of the wild black panther, and copper eyes, the Bombay is a stunning breed

Grooming: * *
Origin: US/UK
Activity: * * * *
GCCF Group: Foreign Shorthairs

Burmilla

The Burmilla is a recent breed that arrived by accident. From this, a whole new range of Burmese-shaped cats developed. This is known as the Asian group (see Asian, Tiffanie, Bombay pages 108, 78 and 112).

Origins The result of an accidental mating in London between a lilac Burmese female and a male Chinchilla owned by Baroness Miranda von Kirchberg, this breed has a romantic origin. The two cats grew up together, designated for different breeding programmes. The Burmese was locked into the study, ready to meet her Burmese mate, when the housekeeper heard the Chinchilla scratching at the door. Thinking the two had been accidentally separated she opened the door. Nature took its course and in 1981 the first Burmillas arrived!

Appearance A cat of Burmese type, well muscled, sturdy but elegant. The difference is the coat, which has inherited the tipped shading of the Chinchilla ancestor. The undercoat is pale, with even tipping over the rest of the body and with a distinct 'M' on the forehead. Colours are black, blue, chocolate, lilac, caramel and apricot, in both full and Burmese expression.

Foreign Shorthair group

Temperament This was the first breed to have 'temperament' written into its Standard of Points – when the breeding programme was set up the aim was to produce a cat that would be both beautiful and sweet natured. Intelligent, lively and friendly, it is quieter than the Burmese but more outgoing than the Chinchilla.

Suitability as a pet The Burmilla makes a great family pet. It gets on well with other breeds and other family pets. In a rural environment it is a great hunter.

Recent additions to the Burmilla programme include the Brown Tipped (left) and the Chocolate Silver Shaded (right)

Grooming: **
Origin: UK
Activity: ****
GCCF Group: Foreign Shorthairs

Cornish Rex

One of the 'curly-coated' varieties of cat, the Cornish Rex is established worldwide, where it has long enjoyed full championship status. An elegant breed that looks as if it has been taken to the hairdresser's and given a perm!

Origins A local farmer first spotted a curly-coated kitten in Cornwall, England, in the 1950s. This aroused the attention of the local vet, since the mother and siblings were all smooth coated. At the vet's suggestion, the curly-coated male was mated back to his mother, resulting in two more kittens with curly coats. The appearance of the curly coat was accepted as a natural mutation, and a breeding programme was devised to ensure the survival of the breed. The 'rex' suffix was added as a description of the coat, after the curly coat already seen in Rex rabbits.

Appearance A medium-sized, well-muscled but slender cat, with a long, wedge-shaped head, large, high-set ears and a long, tapering tail. The coat is short, soft in texture, with curly waves that give a rippled effect. The Cornish Rex is available in all coat colours and patterns, including the Siamese (himalayan) pattern.

Temperament A lively, active and intelligent breed that is quite talkative. Inquisitive by nature, the Cornish Rex character is often described as 'naughty but nice'.

Suitability as a pet With its outgoing personality, the Cornish Rex suits even the busiest of households. It loves the company of children, cats and other pets. As a breed with less fur than most, the paler varieties need to have vulnerable points, such as the ears, treated with sun block if they are to be exposed to sunlight. You should watch their diet too – Cornish have hearty appetites and are prone to obesity.

The Cornish Rex comes in a multitude of colours, as seen in this mixed litter of reds and torties

Grooming: *
Origin: UK
Activity: * * * * *
GCCF Group: Foreign Shorthairs

Devon Rex

Another curly-coated breed, the mischievous Devon Rex is popular in all the cat fancies. With its large bat-like ears and impish expression, the Devon Rex is often referred to as the 'ET of the cat world'!

Origins In the 1960s, a decade after the discovery of the Cornish Rex, another curly-coated kitten was born in the neighbouring county of Devon. At first, it was thought to be the result of the same genetic mutation but this theory was disproved when the two apparently similar types of cat were mated together and produced normally coated kittens. Thus, another new breed had naturally occurred and was named the Devon Rex.

Appearance Smaller, and with less dense hair than the Cornish, it has a full-cheeked, wedge-shaped head with large eyes and large, low-set ears. The ears give the breed its hallmark pixie-like face. It is seen in all coat colours and patterns, including the Siamese pattern.

Temperament Mischievous, friendly, talkative and playful, the Devon Rex is one of the most active breeds of cat. Indeed, it rarely sits still and will quite simply be interested in anything and everything.

Suitability as a pet A companionable breed that loves being with people and other animals, the Devon will not enjoy being in a household where it is left alone for long periods of time. As with the Cornish, protection with sun block should be provided for the ears of paler-coloured cats during summer months. This is another greedy breed, so watch the food intake and waistline.

*Available in a multitude of colours and patterns, the Devon Rex is seen in (**right**) Lilac Silver tabby, one of the paler colours and (**left**) the more deeply coloured brown tabby*

Grooming: *
Country of Origin: UK
Activity: * * * * *
GCCF Group: Foreign Shorthairs

Egyptian Mau

An elegant, foreign-typed, spotted breed, the Egyptian Mau strongly resembles cats seen in Egyptian art that adorns the walls of pharaohs' tombs.

Origins In the 1960s Angela Sayer, a UK breeder, sought to breed an Oriental cat with the spotted coat of the early Egyptian cats. The result was the Egyptian Mau. To avoid confusion with the 'true' Egyptian Mau, a US breed, the UK version was re-named the Oriental Spotted Tabby (see page 149). In the US, the breed's modern history dates back to the Egyptian Embassy in Rome in the early 1950s. Maus were brought over from their native country and became the Embassy's mascots. In 1956 three cats from this line were brought to the US, where a breeding line was established to promote this ancient breed. It has only recently arrived in the UK.

Appearance Elegant, with a modified wedge-shaped head, the Mau is less extreme than the Siamese, and has a body similar to the Abyssinian's. The coat consists of black spots overlying a tabby base colour of bronze, silver or smoke. Newer colours are being bred, such as black and blue, but not all of these are yet recognized.

Foreign Shorthair group

Temperament An intelligent breed with a lively, affectionate and outgoing nature. Less noisy than some foreign-type cats, Maus will still enjoy having a chat with their owners, to whom they become quite devoted.

Suitability as a pet The Mau enjoys a family environment and the company of other cats and pets. Their bossy character can dominate a household. They love the outdoors and can become good hunters.

The best-known colour for a Mau is silver. This cat shows the colour to perfection

Grooming: *
Country of Origin: Egypt/US/UK
Activity: *
GCCF Group: Foreign Shorthair (provisional)

Japanese Bobtail

Revered in Japan, this breed is distinguished by its short, curled tail. It is accepted in the US, where it is popular, but not worldwide. It is virtually unknown in the UK.

Origins Although the exact background of this ancient breed is not well documented, it is thought to originate in China or Southeast Asia, rather than Japan. How it arrived in Japan is open to speculation, but it is in this country that it has become established, and is known as the 'Mi-Ke', traditionally a tri-coloured cat symbolizing friendship and good fortune. Imported into the US in the late 1960s, Japanese Bobtails were granted full status in that country a decade later.

Appearance Slender and dainty, this is a well-muscled, medium-sized breed whose hind legs are longer than its forelegs. In this respect it is reminiscent of another breed that has an island origin, the Manx. The most distinctive feature is the short, bobbed tail, which lays curled when the cat is resting but is upright when the cat moves. The classic coat pattern is that of the tri-coloured Mi-Ke, although other colours and patterns are also now accepted.

Temperament Affectionate, intelligent, lively and companionable, with a voice that is said to have a unique melodic chant.

Suitability as a pet Generally undemanding, this breed makes a good family pet. A longhaired variety is available – be prepared for a considerable amount of grooming if you choose this.

Right The most distinctive feature of the Japanese Bobtail is the short, curled tail

Left Although popular in the US, this breed has only recently been imported into the UK

Grooming: * *
Country of Origin: Southeast Asia/Japan
Activity: * * *
GCCF Group: unrecognized

Korat

An old breed, the Korat is one of the few one-colour varieties. It is an elegant cat with a slate-blue coat and a sweet expression. The breed is still relatively rare.

Origins Native to Thailand, where it is known as 'Si-Sawat', the Korat is considered sacred and a bringer of good fortune. References to this breed are found in early Thai history, but the first recorded evidence of the Korat in the West was in 1896, when one was reportedly exhibited at a cat show in London. After this they faded from the show scene. The Korat that we see today is the result of a breeding programme set up in the 1950s in the US using cats imported from Thailand. They did not reach the UK again until the 1970s.

Appearance Although reports of a dilute lilac Korat have been noted, this has never been accepted as a true colour variation of the breed. The Korat that graces the show benches today is only recognized in the traditional blue. Medium-sized and muscular, this breed has a heart-shaped face with large, lustrous eyes. The coat is close-lying and smooth, but has an unusual trait in that it is 'broken', or slightly up-standing, along the spine.

Foreign Shorthair group

Temperament An intelligent breed that is loving, gentle and quiet-voiced.

Suitability as a pet Although an active breed, the Korat has a placid nature and will usually prefer to live in a quiet household, without too many noisy intrusions.

Right As with any young animal, Korat kittens often go through a 'gangly' stage, but they soon grow into those ears!

Left The heart-shaped face and large eyes give the Korat its appealing expression

Grooming: * *
Origin: Thailand
Activity: * * *
GCCF Group: Foreign Shorthairs

Ocicat

One of the more recently developed spotted Tabby breeds, the Ocicat has great appeal. So-called because it resembles a small Ocelot, it has a firm following in the US and its popularity is increasing in the UK and the rest of Europe.

Origins This breed was created by accident. In the 1960s a US breeder was trying to produce a Siamese cat with Abyssinian points. A cross-mating between a Siamese Seal Point and a half Abyssinian resulted in a litter of assorted tabbies. One rather special little kitten was noticed, a golden-coloured, spotted Tabby, and it was given the name 'Tonga'. Generally considered to be the first Ocicat, Tonga was exhibited only once, at a cat show in 1985. His striking colour and pattern were so much admired, as he resembled a little wild cat, that a breeding programme was created to continue the line.

Appearance A large, solid, well-muscled breed of non-extreme type, with a broad head, squarish muzzle and large, wide-set, tufted ears. The most obvious attraction of the Ocicat is its coat pattern, which should be well spotted with a banded tail. Colours are recognized in brown, blue, chocolate, lilac, cinnamon, fawn, red, cream, torbie and the silvers of these colours.

Foreign Shorthair group

Temperament Although generally affectionate and undemanding, it may be cautious of strangers, wisely perhaps, since its coat makes it a target for cat thieves.

Suitability as a pet In general, Ocicats get on well with all pets. Given a free-range lifestyle, the Ocicat will become a great hunter and enjoy being outside. Some Ocicats have sensitive hearing, so a fairly quiet household would probably be most suitable.

*Ocicats are quite new to the UK, and this Chocolate (**left**) and Black Silver (**right**) show the markings required of the breed*

Grooming: * *
Origin: US
Activity: * * * *
GCCF Group: Foreign Shorthairs

Russian Blue

This breed's grace has led to it being compared with a ballerina dancing 'en pointe'. Its thick, double coat reflects its northern origins; this, combined with the silvery-blue colour of the coat, makes it quite enchanting.

Origins The Russian Blue was originally known as the 'Archangel Cat', as it is thought to have originated from the north Russian port of Arkhangel'sk. The cats probably found their way to Europe, particularly the UK, via nineteenth-century sailors trading from Baltic ports. They may have arrived earlier than this, travelling as 'ratters' on the Viking longships. The Russian Blue was exhibited in UK cat shows in the late 1800s. After that, its popularity waned until it was resurrected in the 1950s by the use of outcrosses to Siamese.

Appearance A medium-sized cat with long, slender legs, the Russian should exude grace and elegance. The head has a straight profile with a flat skull and large, high-set ears. Although both white and black Russians have been seen, most likely arriving from the temporary Siamese outcrosses, only Blue is currently recognized.

Foreign Shorthair group

Temperament Although quiet-voiced, placid and sensitive, the Russian is a playful cat that will enjoy gentle companionship from a family.

Suitability as a pet In general, the Russian will not enjoy a loud, busy household with active, noisy children. It is really a grown-up's cat, and likes quiet nights in. If a cat was a music lover, it would appreciate Mozart rather than Wagner – and would probably do the crossword while enjoying a glass of port!

The gentle natured Russian Blue, a one-colour only breed, has distinctive high-set ears

Grooming: **
Origin: Russia
Activity: ***
GCCF Group: Foreign Shorthairs

Singapura

This dainty, attractive cat is one of the smaller breeds. What it lacks in size, however, it certainly makes up for in personality. This has to be one of the most people-orientated cats ever bred – it just loves everyone it meets.

Origins It is thought that similar cats existed in Singapore 300 years ago. The modern Singapura traces back to the early 1970s, when a US serviceman brought three back to the US. His wife, a cat breeder, recognized the potential of this petite, sweet-natured cat and, with the help of further imports, started to develop the breed. By the 1980s Singapuras had gained official recognition in the US and, in 1988, were imported into the UK where they initially received little enthusiasm. In 1993, a breeder in the UK, Debbie van den Berg, re-kindled the interest and formed a club dedicated to this breed.

Appearance Although smaller than many breeds, the Singapura is a strong, muscular but elegant cat that feels heavier than it looks. The head is rounded with a blunt muzzle, with large, pointed ears and large, lustrous eyes. The smooth, silky coat is available in sepia agouti colour only – a warm ivory overlaid with sepia brown ticking.

Temperament This cat has two speeds: fast forward and stop. Inquisitive and loving, it will be into everything. It is fond of sitting on its owner's shoulders.

Suitability as a pet The Singapura is probably best suited to a lively and athletic household; even as it gets older it keeps up its kitten-like activities. Singapuras are fascinated by high places and will often be found on the tops of doors and wardrobes. They can also be rather clumsy so ornaments should be watched!

The diminutive Singapura is a sweet-natured breed

Grooming: * *
Origin: Singapore
Activity: * * * * *
GCCF Group: Foreign Shorthairs

Snowshoe

A rare breed developed in the US during the 1960s, the attractively patterned Snowshoe has a small, but growing and dedicated following.

Origins The first Snowshoes were the result of crossing a Siamese with a Bi-colour American Shorthair. Mating one of these kittens back to a Siamese gave a shorthaired, blue-eyed litter with Siamese points and the trademark white 'boots'. A campaign was subsequently established in the US to develop and promote the breed and in the 1980s the Snowshoe was granted championship status there.

Appearance Combining the graceful shape and colour pattern of the Siamese with the muscularity of the American Shorthair, the Snowshoe is an elegant, medium-to-large-sized breed. The short coats have a paler body colour than the points, and are recognized in all colours accepted for the Siamese. The head is a moderate wedge, never as extreme as the Siamese's, and – for perfection – there should be an inverted 'V' of white from the bridge of the nose to between the eyes.

Temperament Intelligent, inquisitive, friendly and athletic, the Snowshoe is a sweet-natured breed that combines the best personality traits from its ancestors – the extrovert, outgoing Siamese and the laid-back Shorthair. An excellent recipe for the perfect pet.

Suitability as a pet A companionable breed that would suit almost any household, the Snowshoe seems to adapt to any domestic situation and enjoys the company of humans, cats and other pets alike.

Above The Lilac snowshoe is one of the paler colours

Above right The Harlequin Seal Tortie Point is a striking pattern of this breed

Grooming: * *
Origin: US
Activity: * * *
GCCF Group: unrecognized

Sphynx

It's a fallacy that the Sphynx is a bald cat. It has a soft, downy coat that feels rather like the surface of a peach or a piece of soft chamois leather. This unusual cat has the most remarkable, fun-loving personality.

Origins In 1966 a nearly hairless kitten was born to a Canadian domestic cat. Although the US recognized the Sphynx in 1971, its popularity dwindled. Meanwhile, interest was growing in Europe, particularly France and Holland. This led to new Sphynx breeding programmes and today it is popular throughout the US and most of Europe, with a dedicated, small band of breeders campaigning for its status in the UK.

Appearance Different, to say the least! It has been described as bald, wrinkled and 'the cat in its birthday suit'. Despite this, the Sphynx is an elegant, well-muscled cat with long, slim legs. The large, wide-set ears are a prominent feature but it is the lack of coat that makes the breed distinctive. Available in all colours, the pattern and pigmentation should be clearly visible, with some wrinkles, although these should not be extreme.

Foreign Shorthair group

Temperament Sweet natured, friendly, amusing, acrobatic and mischievous, these cats are clowns that just love entertaining everyone they meet.

Suitability as a pet This breed requires no grooming, but must be protected with sun block if it goes out in the sun. It enjoys the company of its owners and other pets. With little fur, it has less dander (flakes of skin similar to dandruff) – ideal for the allergic cat lover.

A graceful and elegant breed, the Sphynx may not have much to show off in the fur department, but it is a breed with personality – plus!

Grooming: *
Origin: Canada
Activity: * * *
GCCF Group: unrecognized

Tonkinese

This is a breed resulting from a mating between the Burmese and Siamese breeds, and enjoys the characteristics of both these breeds in modified form. The Tonkinese is popular with those who seek a cat reminiscent of the 'old-fashioned' Siamese, but that is less extreme and with a rounder head shape.

Origins On the one hand, the Tonkinese was created by the mating of a Siamese with a Burmese, producing a hybrid. On the other hand, it is documented that the original Burmese (see page 154) was a hybrid, probably with a history that included Siamese. The modern Tonkinese was originally created in the US, but it was in Canada that it was finally recognized as a distinct breed, and it is now accepted by most cat fancies.

Appearance In type, the Tonkinese fits in quite happily between the elongated Siamese and the rounder-shaped Burmese. Medium-sized, muscular and lithe, this breed has a coat colour that lies midway between that of its original parentage – neither self nor pointed, it has a more graduated shading. Today the coat is accepted in all colours and shades, including tortie and tabby.

Foreign Shorthair group

Temperament This breed is outgoing, lively and sociable. It is a 'chatty' cat but not to the extent of its more vociferous ancestors.

Suitability as a pet As with most mixed-breed varieties, the Tonkinese will suit most domestic situations. It gets on well with other cats and animals and enjoys general household hubbub. Its short coat needs little more than a regular brush and comb.

The 'halfway-house' between Siamese and Burmese, the Tonkinese is available in many colours

Grooming: * *
Origin: US/Canada
Activity: * * *
GCCF Group: Foreign Shorthairs

Oriental Shorthair group

A 'genetically engineered' breed of cat, the Oriental is basically a group of cats with the shape of the Siamese but without the restricted himalayan points. This group is the only one that does not have a history relating to a particular country of origin.

The Havana, a deep-chestnut-coloured cat, is probably the best known of this group today. However, the breeders were originally aiming to create a chocolate-coloured Siamese. They mated a Seal Point Siamese to a Russian Blue and the resulting black kittens were then mated back to Siamese in the hope that the required chocolate colour might result. During the same period a Seal Point Siamese mis-mated with a half Siamese and, as luck would have it, a chocolate-coloured kitten was found in the litter. From these two original lines, the deep-chestnut-coloured cat that we now call the Havana evolved.

But this was just the beginning. Mating back to Siamese, many carrying the dilute gene, meant it was possible to breed blues and lilacs. Crossing Siamese to a white shorthair, and then crossing the progeny back to Siamese, eventually produced the Foreign White. Outcrosses involving the red-, cream- and tortie-pointed Siamese gave rise to the original colours of self-reds, cream and torties but also produced the dilute colours of chocolate, caramel, cinnamon and fawn. From matings to the tabby-pointed series of Siamese the most popular Oriental Tabbies evolved. By adding silver to the mix (originated by introducing the Chinchilla Persian) another whole spectrum of colours became available.

What started out as an idea to breed a self-colour cat of Siamese shape but without the colour restrictions has therefore resulted in a vast selection of cats. Orientals are available in almost any colour, shade and pattern imaginable.

Origins Self-coloured Siamese have been in evidence for many years, the result of a Siamese mis-mating with a cat of unknown parentage. In the UK it was not until the 1950s that experimental matings took place in an attempt to produce self-coloured cats. Today this is probably the most rapidly expanding group of all known breeds, as different colours, along with their patterned relations, are constantly being produced.

Appearance Essentially, these are self or patterned cats of exactly the same body conformation as the Siamese – they just don't have points. Both elegant and angular in body shape with long, slender legs and proportionately long tails, the Orientals have broad, wedge-shaped heads with wide-set ears, almond-shaped eyes (classically green in colour, except with the white varieties) and long, slender necks. In profile, the head is quite straight, without any stop or break. The overall impression of the Oriental is one of a well-muscled, graceful and evenly balanced cat, with a bright and intelligent expression.

The Oriental Spotted Tabby has particularly distinctive markings

Oriental Shorthair group

Temperament Orientals have the character as well as the body shape of a Siamese. Intelligent, friendly and inquisitive, this is a loving breed that demands attention – and will ask for it in a loud voice if its requests are not met!

Suitability as a pet The Oriental's short, sleek coat needs little by way of grooming and from this point of view the breed could be considered low maintenance. The Oriental is fun loving and into everything and anything, including everyday household activities such as bed making and washing up! Retrieving is a favourite sport – it loves to bring back toys that have been thrown for it to fetch. Orientals enjoy a family environment and will get along well with other pets, as long as things aren't overcrowded. Like the Siamese, they need their own space.

Grooming: *
Origin: UK
Activity: * * * *
GCCF Group: Oriental Shorthairs

Variations

Havana

Despite its name, the Havana has no relation to Cuba, being a breed first developed in the UK in the 1950s. This variation has an even, warm, chestnut-coloured coat that was officially recognized in the UK in 1958. A similar but genetically unrelated breed, the Havana Brown, exists in the US.

Left The Havana was one of the first colours of Oriental to be recognized in the UK

Right A typical feature of the Havana is the bright, clear green eyes

Black

Although 'black' Siamese were reputedly seen in Germany before the Second World War, the Oriental Black that we see today is the result of the Oriental breeding programme. One of the most eye-catching of the self-coloured Orientals, the Black has a sleek, glossy, black coat.

Left *The head of the Oriental should resemble a triangle, with wide-set ears and a long muzzle*

Right *Long, lithe and angular, this Oriental Black shows all the class and elegance required of the breed*

Blue (and Lilac)

The Blue has a medium-to-light-blue coat, but, unlike the Burmese, no silvering is seen in the coat. The Lilac is a paler version of the Blue, with a frosty-grey coat that shows a pinkish tinge.

Right *This Oriental Blue's expression sums up the intelligence and inquisitive nature so typical of the breed*

Below *The coat of any Oriental should be sleek and close-lying*

Red

This variety has a rich, warm-red coat that should be as even in colour as possible.

Left A particular feature of the Oriental is the long, slender legs

Below The warm, rich red coat is allowed to show slight tabby markings

Cream

Slightly lighter in colour than the Red, the Cream Oriental has a cool-cream-coloured coat.

Left *A difficult colour variation to breed with a clear coat, the Oriental Cream is not penalized for having some faint tabby patterns visible*

Below *The Cream should have vivid green eyes – the deeper the colour, the better*

White

With a glacial-white coat, this variety of Oriental has
brilliant blue eyes.

Left This variety has
a pure white coat,
with no trace of
shading

Below And the deep,
clear, brilliant blue eyes
make this a dazzling
variety of Oriental

New colours

Although not all of these are recognized worldwide, new colours include cinnamon, caramel, apricot and fawn.

Left The Caramel Shaded Oriental is a welcome addition to the new spectrum of Oriental colours. . .

Below . . . . as is the Self Cinnamon

Tabby – Spotted

Originally known as the Egyptian Mau in the UK (but quite distinct from the breed now known by this name – see page 120), this is probably the most glamorous of all the Tabby varieties within this group. Available in a wide range of colours, it is most important that the coat should show well-defined spots overlying the paler, agouti background.

Right With the pale-coloured Lilac Spotted Tabby Oriental the pattern is often difficult to see . . .

Below . . . whereas the richer colour of the red shows off the spotted pattern to perfection

Tabby – Classic

The Classic Tabby has an agouti background overlaid with swirls of a darker colour, silver being one of the most common. It is available in all the colours seen in the self varieties, although not all colours are recognized worldwide.

Left The profile for the Oriental should always be long and straight

Right It is important that the markings show a good contrast, with obvious 'butterflies' on the shoulders and 'oyster' patterns on the flanks

Tabby – Ticked

First granted championship status in the UK in 1993, the Ticked Tabby developed from a mating between Siamese and Abyssinian cats. The coat, which comes in a variety of colours, should be evenly ticked with at least two or three bands of colour on each strand of hair.

Left The delicate pattern of the paler varieties, such as this Cream Ticked, show how subtle colours and patterns can mix together

Right Added to the tabby pattern and overlaid with silver, this makes for a very spectacular feline indeed

Tortie

The Tortie is usually a female-only variety and has a coat of any of the accepted self colours intermingled with either red or cream. When this coat is combined with the tabby pattern, the resulting cat is the Tortie Tabby, also known as the Torbie or Torby.

The Oriental is an elegant breed, as this Chocolate Ticked Tortie demonstrates

Shaded (and Smoke)

These subtle patterns are available in all the colours recognized in the self colours; the Smoke has an evenly coloured over-mantle while the Shaded is similar, but displays the agouti pattern.

Left A newer colour, the Chocolate Silver shaded has a clear, pale silver undercoat, overlaid with Chocolate Agouti

Below The Caramel Shaded has a cool, pale beige undercoat with Caramel ticking

Burmese group
(US: some colours called Malayan)

Another of the most popular groups of pedigree cat, the Burmese is internationally recognized and currently rates fourth on the registration list in the UK. Though neither as glamorous or distinctively marked as its Siamese relations, the Burmese has personality plus and its people-orientated character has gained it a firm following within both the Cat Fancy and with pet owners.

Often described as the 'dog cat', the Burmese will follow its owner with almost dog-like devotion – but with a proportionate sense of feline humour. While Burmese adore company (this is a breed that gets on with anybody and any animal), they also have a serious 'don't mess with me' attitude and need to be treated with the respect they deserve.

The type of Burmese varies quite radically between the US and the UK. In the former they tend to be of a much cobbier overall type, with a distinctively rounded head, which is often described as an 'apple head'. These traits are far less apparent in the UK, where the standards require a

Burmese group

cat with an elegantly balanced shape, and in general a more modified and less extreme appearance than its US counterpart. Terminology also varies between the US and UK. The US terms for the original colours – sable, champagne and platinum – were replaced in the UK by brown, chocolate and lilac; conversely, the colours developed in the UK, such as red, cream and tortie, are regarded as a different breed – the Malayan – in the US.

Although the Burmese is best known as a self-coated cat, in fact this is not strictly speaking a self variety. Self cats have kittens that are born the same colour as the adult. Burmese kittens, however, are born a very pale colour. At birth, it can be difficult to decide what colour

Brown, blue and lilac are just some of the colours available in the Burmese group, as seen in this large litter of kittens

the kittens will become in adulthood and, in the early days of the blues, chocolates and lilacs, it was not unknown for a cat to be re-registered (some times twice or more) as a different colour.

At the end of the day, however, it does not matter at all what name the cat is given – a Burmese will always be a Burmese.

A mixture of lilac and cream, with matching nose leather, the Lilac Tortie Burmese is the palest of the tortie varieties

Burmese group

The Brown Tortie Burmese was the original colour of tortie, first seen in the UK

Origins It is well documented that the first 'Burmese' was a little brown cat named Wong Mau that was brought from the Far East (probably Burma) to the west coast of the US in 1930. It is open to debate as to whether she was a true Burmese or a hybrid – indeed, it is often said that she was what is now considered to be a Tonkinese. As there were no similarly coloured cats available to mate her with, she was mated to a Siamese and the resulting kittens were obviously hybrids. A generation later, mating one of her male kittens of similar colour back to her meant the progeny then included kittens of similar appearance and colour. These are what are generally regarded as the first Burmese cats and Dr Thompson, the owner of Wong Mau, continued breeding cats from these original lines. It was not until 1948 that Burmese arrived in the UK. Other colours developed: in the US the Chocolate (Champagne) and Lilac (Platinum); in the UK the Blue arrived by natural mutation and later the Red, Cream and Torties were created by a dedicated band of breeders in the UK.

Appearance The Burmese is a medium-sized cat, sturdy and well muscled. It is neither as slender as the Siamese nor as heavily boned as the British. The head is rounded, displaying, for perfection, a domed skull with wide-set, medium-sized ears. In profile the nose should display a distinct break and the chin should be firm. The golden-coloured eyes are almond-shaped and expressive; overall, these cats have an expression that is often described as 'wicked', but this could just as easily refer to their wicked sense of humour.

Burmese group

Temperament This is a breed that loves its owner to death; it wants to be with you all the time and enjoy joining in with your activities.

Suitability as a pet Although the Burmese is generally a gregarious breed that enjoys the company of both humans, cats and dogs, it does not like to be overcrowded – a Burmese needs its own space. With too many cats in a multi-cat household, a Burmese can become territorial and this can lead these usually sweet-natured, friendly and clean cats to display distinctly anti-social behaviour.

Grooming: *
Origin: Burma
Activity: * * * * *
GCCF Group: Burmese

Variations

Brown (US: Sable)

The glossy, short, close-lying coat should be of an even, warm, deep brown and free of any obvious barring or shading (although these markings are permissible in kittens).

Left The Burmese should have a dome between the ears

Right Given the opportunity, the athletic and active Burmese will love access to a garden

Blue

A natural mutation originally seen in the UK, the first Blue Burmese was born in 1955 and, rather aptly, named Sealcoat Blue Surprise. This welcome addition has a soft, silvery-grey coat, with the silvering most distinct on the face, ears and paws.

Left Burmese are natural born adventurers, so if allowed to go outside it is prudent to ensure they wear a collar

Right A UK show champion, this Blue Burmese shows all the finer points of the breed

Chocolate (US: Champagne)

First seen in the US, the Chocolate Burmese is paler than the Brown, having a warm, even, milk-chocolate-coloured coat, although a slightly deeper tone is accepted for the face, ears, paws and tail.

Right *The Burmese should have wide cheek bones, and a short blunt muzzle, as this Chocolate Burmese shows nicely*

Left *This Chocolate Burmese was awarded the ultimate accolade in the UK – Supreme Grand Champion*

Lilac (US: Platinum)

With a pale, dove-grey coat that has a distinct pinkish tinge, the Lilac is another colour variation that originally came from the US.

Left Although the coat colour of the Lilac should be as even as possible, it is quite acceptable for the face to be a slightly darker colour

Right The general conformation of the Burmese is of a medium-sized, well-muscled cat with a strong, rounded chest

Red

The Red Burmese (along with the associated Cream and torties) was a purely UK-based invention, resulting from a breeding programme instigated in the mid-1960s by Joyce Dell and Robine Pocock, with the help of the Burmese Cat Club. The Red has a rich, light-tangerine-coloured coat, with darker shadings on the face, ears, legs and paws.

The rich red colouring of the Burmese is a popular variety in the UK, whereas in the US this colour is considered as a Malayan

Cream

The dilute version of the Red, the Cream has an attractive, pale-cream-coloured coat that has a distinct 'powdery' look on the face, ears and paws.

Subtly paler than the red, the Burmese is also seen in cream .... a colour first developed in England

Brown Tortie

As with any breed displaying this coat pattern, the Burmese Tortie is usually a female-only variety. The Brown Tortie has a coat that displays an intermingled mixture of red, cream and brown.

Right *This little brown Tortie kitten displays the inquisitive expression so associated with this breed*

Left *This variety should show a good mixture of red, cream and brown colours in the coat*

Blue Tortie

Originally named the Blue Cream, the Blue Tortie Burmese has a coat that combines blue and cream colours.

Right In profile, the Burmese should have a good nose break

Left The Burmese is an alert breed by nature

Chocolate Tortie

This attractive variation has a coat of pale chocolate intermingled with cream.

Left Regardless of colour or pattern, the Burmese should always look ready for action

Right Elegant and lithe, this chocolate tortie displays all the characteristics required of the breed

Lilac Tortie

The palest of all the torties, the Lilac Tortie's coat is a mixture of lilac and cream.

The palest of all the torties, the lilac shows a well-mingled coat of lilac and cream

Siamese group
(US: some colours called Colorpoint Shorthair)

With their distinctive pale coats highlighted with the darker himalayan points and their eyes of a clear, vivid blue, Siamese just exude class and elegance. Along with the Persians, this breed was one of the first recognized pedigree cats. From the original 'Royal Cat of Siam', a pale-coated cat with dark, seal-brown points, the Siamese today is bred in almost every colour imaginable. Charming, intelligent and companionable, these cats make delightful pets but can also be somewhat demanding of both your time and attention.

When Siamese first arrived in the UK in the 1880s, these slimly built cats were often considered to have a somewhat frail and delicate constitution. This is hardly surprising, as they had come from a very warm climate to a very cold, damp one. Equally, they became exposed to different bugs and diseases and the natural immunity they had built up to viruses in their homeland no longer served them well.

Siamese group

Early Siamese were indeed a difficult breed to rear successfully, as the kittens were prone to all sorts of infections. Through the dedication of the early breeders and the advance in knowledge of veterinary science, however, these cats soon overcame their original health problems and today Siamese are no more susceptible to infections than any other breed of cat. Indeed, many Siamese in the UK have been known to live to celebrate their twenty-first birthdays – not bad going for any cat!

Seal Point is the original colour and still one of the most popular

Accepted as a Colorpoint Shorthair in the US, this Tortie Point Siamese displays all the elegance required of the breed

In the UK a simple system was established to separate two quite distinct breeding lines. The original Siamese colours are registered under breed number 24 and include seal, blue, chocolate and lilac; all other colours and patterns are classified as breed 32. A similar system exists in the US, where the seal, blue, chocolate and frost (lilac) points are regarded as Siamese, and all other colours and patterns classified as Colorpoint Shorthair.

Siamese group

Origin As the name would suggest, Siamese cats originated in Siam (now Thailand), where they were regarded as sacred cats. Early Siamese displayed two traits that are considered severe faults for the modern show-quality Siamese: tail kinks and squinted eyes. Although these features have been successfully bred out of modern lines, the curious legends remain. One legend is that a pair of Siamese was sent off to find and return a valuable goblet that had been stolen from a Buddhist temple. After many days of travel the goblet was found. Although both cats were tired, the male returned to the temple to relay the news while his lady stayed to keep guard of the treasure. She wrapped her long tail around the precious object tightly, watching it with devout attention and to the extent that her tail became kinked and her eyes acquired a permanent squint. Some weeks later, she gave birth to a litter of kittens, all with kinked tails and eye squints. Another legend tells of a Siamese princess who used her cat's tail as a place for the safe keeping of her valuable rings. One night, the cat fell asleep and the rings were lost. The angry princess tied a knot in the tail to ensure that this never happened again.

Appearance The Siamese is a muscular cat that has a long, lean, slim and elegant body with a very angular shape. The head is an almost perfect triangle; at the top, the large ears are set wide on the skull, the cheeks are broad and narrow to a fine muzzle. In profile the head is long and straight, with no nose break or stop. The points, restricted to the mask, ears, legs and tail, should show a clear contrast to the paler body colour.

Tabby (Lynx in the US) has been a popular addition to the group

Siamese group

Temperament The Siamese has an outgoing, larger-than-life character, which is one of the reasons the breed is so popular. Highly affectionate, the Siamese is intelligent and likes to declare in a loud voice that it is part of the family.

Suitability as a pet With their close-lying, sleek fur, these cats will not require you to spend much time on grooming – they can do it on their own. The Siamese is a very active breed and can be somewhat demanding; this is a breed that will instigate a conversation, rather than just quietly reply to a question. Extremely active and inquisitive, Siamese will fit into most households, including those with pets and children. Although the Siamese is most charming, do not be tempted to keep too many of them. In an overcrowded feline environment these cats tend to display territorial habits, including spraying – you have been warned!

Grooming: *
Origin: Siam (Thailand)
Activity: * * * * *
GCCF Group: Siamese

Variations

Seal Point

The original 'Royal Cat of Siam', this variation should have points that are a dark seal-brown with a pale cream body colour.

Left Type can vary between the US and UK. This is an American Seal Point Siamese

Below Whereas this is a classic example of the standards required for the UK show bench

Blue Point

Originally thought of as a poorly coloured Seal Point, the Blue Point was first seen at a show in 1896. Receiving recognition in the UK in 1939, today this variety has light blue points overlaid on a glacial-white body colour.

Left The Siamese should have a head that is triangular in shape

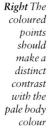

Right The coloured points should make a distinct contrast with the pale body colour

Chocolate Point

First recorded in 1931, this was another variety that has been described as a badly coloured Seal Point. Finally accepted for championship status in 1950, the Chocolate Point has a pale-ivory body colour with warm, milk-chocolate-coloured points.

Left The Chocolate Point is allowed to have paler legs than other varieties of Siamese

Below This Chocolate Point shows the points off to perfection

Lilac Point (US: Frost Point)

This variety has a glacial-white body, with delicate pinkish-grey points.

Left Its brilliant blue eyes are one of the most striking features of the Siamese

Right Slim, lithe and angular, this Lilac Point sums up the elegance of the breed

Red Point
(US: Red Colorpoint Shorthair)

With rich, bright, golden-red coloured points overlaid on a warm, white coat the Red Point was first seen in 1934 and was awarded championship status in the UK some thirty years later in 1966.

Left This Red Point displays the typically large ears of the breed

Below The pale body colour and warmer coloured points are the required standards

Cream Point
(US: Cream Colorpoint Shorthair)

The paler version of the Red Point, this variety was also afforded status in 1966. The Cream Point has cool, cream points with a powdery look, overlaying an even paler cream body colour.

Left The Siamese's profile should be quite straight, as seen in this Cream Point

Right The nose leather is a pale, flesh-colour pink to match the pale cream coat

Tortie Point
(US: Tortie Colorpoint Shorthair)

This is the usually female-only pattern within this group and is acceptable in any of the main pointed colours, intermingled with red, cream or a mixture of both.

Left Tortie Point Siamese are available in a multitude of colours

Below This Seal Tortie Point won Best in Show at the centenary show of the UK's Siamese Cat Club

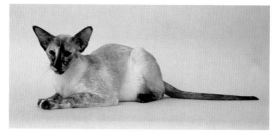

Tabby Point
(US: Lynx Colorpoint Shorthair)

A most popular variation of Siamese pattern, the Tabby Point is available in a variety of colours, including Tortie-Tabby (Torbie/Torby).

Left The Chocolate Tabby Point is one of the most popular amongst this breed

Below The Caramel Tabby Point is one of the newer variations

New colours

More recently, new Colourpoints of Siamese have been developed, including caramel, fawn, cinnamon and apricot.

*Through more recent breeding programmes, even more dilute colours have become available including (**left**) the Fawn Point and (**below**) the Apricot Point*

Glossary of terms

Agouti Coats with banded striations along each hair shaft, giving rise to different colours and patterns, and typical of the coat found in Tabbies.

Bi-colour A coat that is a well-defined mixture of white and any of the accepted self colours.

Break A distinct dip between the eyes and the nose tip, rather like the bridge of the nose in humans, and which can be seen in profile. This is an important feature in some breeds, including Burmese.

Calico The US term for a Tortie and White, i.e. a coat with a well-defined mixture of white and any of the accepted tortie colours.

Cobby One of the types of cat, cobby is a chunky type, such as the British Shorthair.

Colorpoint Shorthair The US term for certain colours of Siamese.

Colourpoint The UK term for Himalayan, i.e. a Persian cat with the restricted coat pattern of the Siamese.

Colourpointed The UK term for British Shorthaired cats with the restricted coat pattern of the Siamese.

Conformation The basic shape and size of the cat.

Double coat A very heavy undercoat that acts as an insulating layer, plus a lighter topcoat. Most commonly seen in cats that come from colder climates, such as the Russian Blue and Manx.

Extreme/non-extreme When pedigree cats were first seen they really only varied from each other in terms of fur length and colour pattern. Today cats differ from each other in terms of shape. Persians have short faces and Siamese long ones. These two types are know as 'extreme' and most other breeds as 'non-extreme'.

F1 etc A genetic term relating to the first generation cross of two different breeds. F2 = second generation, F3 = third generation etc. Usually used for early generations of new breeds, such as the Bengal.

Full or Burmese expression These are terms that relate only to the Burmilla/Asian breed, which is genetically a very complicated type of cat. The Burmese colour restriction modifies the full expression colour resulting in a black becoming a brown, etc. In other words, the full expression is always a darker version than the Burmese expression.

GCCF The Governing Council of the Cat Fancy. Formed in the UK in 1910, this is the oldest established governing and registering body for pedigree cats, and set the standard for similar organizations in other countries.

Himalayan

i) Himalayan: The genetic term for the restricted colour pattern most commonly seen in the Siamese, i.e. face, legs and tail of a different colour.

ii) Himalayan: The US term for the Colourpoint Longhair (Persian) cat.

Mitted The restricted colour pattern that displays dark colourpoints on the face, ears, tail and legs, but with white paws. Used primarily to describe Ragdolls.

Plumed Describes a full-furred tail in the non-Persian varieties of cat.

Points

i) The restricted colour patterns seen in Siamese, Colourpoints and Himalayans.

ii) The general term regarding the Standard of Points laid down by the relevant governing bodies and used to describe the finer points of a cat's appearance.

Restricted Colour Pattern These are those parts of the body of an otherwise pale-coated animal that show coloured areas. In most cases this includes the face, ears, tail and paws.

Rex The type of curled or wavy fur found in some breeds, such as the Devon Rex and Cornish Rex.

Ruff The fur around the chin and neck area of Longhairs and Semi-Longhairs.

Self Describes a plain-coloured cat that has the colour solid to the roots and with no other colours or shading in the coat.

Solid Another term for self.

Standard of Points The guidelines laid down by the registering bodies to describe and define the way any particular breed of cat should appear. A cat would be judged at a show according to the Points.

Status Championship status allows for a breed to be awarded certificates; newer varieties have to go through preliminary and assessment levels before this is granted.

Tabby A particular coat pattern, which may be classic, spotted or ticked.

Glossary of terms

Tortie Usually a female-only variety, with a mixture of red and/or cream intermingled with one of the accepted self colours.

Ticked Another term for agouti, where each hair is banded in several colours. Most commonly seen in the tabby.

Tipped This term primarily used to describe the Chinchilla, whereby the pale undercoat is lightly tipped in black.

Torbie Also Torby – a cat with a Tortie and Tabby mixed coat.

Tufted Where hair extends out from the top of the ear in 'tufts', which is required in some breeds.

Type The general conformation of the body, as laid down by the governing councils. For example, cobby, foreign, Oriental.

Van A pattern that is seen on white cats with a limited amount of colour restricted to the head and tail. Most commonly seen in the Turkish Van, it is also now accepted for some Persian varieties.

Useful websites

There are so many websites pertaining to cats that any list could become overwhelming. Here, therefore, is a selection of the most useful, all of which have links to other sites that may be more specific to your needs.

Governing/Registering bodies

The Governing Council of the Cat Fancy
www.gccfcats.org

American Cat Fanciers' Association
www.acfacat.com

Canadian Cat Association
www.cca-afc.com

Cat Fanciers' Association
www.cfainc.org

Fédération Internationale Féline
www.fifeweb.org

The International Cat Association (TICA)
www.tica.org

The World Cat Federation (WCF)
www.wcf-online.de/english

Magazines and journals

UK

Our Cats (fortnightly paper that also acts as the official journal for GCCF)

www.ourcats.co.uk

Your Cat (monthly magazine)

www.yourcat.co.uk

US
Cat Fancy
www.catfancy.com

Index of cat breeds